50

Miscellany

Fifty Years of Sunday Miscellany

MISCELLANY 50
First published in 2019 by
New Island Books
16 Priory Office Park
Stillorgan
County Dublin
Republic of Ireland
www.newisland.ie

Print ISBN: 978-1-84840-747-3
eBook ISBN: 978-1-84840-748-0

Song lyric credits: *Hey Ronnie Reagan* © John Maguire (page 64); *Fairytale of New York*
© Shane McGowan and Jem Finer (page 65); *Disco 2000* © Jarvis Cocker (page 167);
The Sea Around Us © Dominic Behan (page 224).

The editor and publisher have made all reasonable effort to trace copyright holders
and obtain permission to reproduce visual material, words and song lyrics. Please
contact the publisher if any copyright appears to have been infringed.

Layout, design and cover design by Catherine Gaffney
Edited by Djinn von Noorden
Printed by L&C Printing Group, Poland

New Island Books is a member of Publishing Ireland.
10 9 8 7 6 5 4 3 2

Miscellany 50

Fifty Years of Sunday Miscellany

Edited by
Clíodhna Ní Anluain

NEW ISLAND

CONTENTS

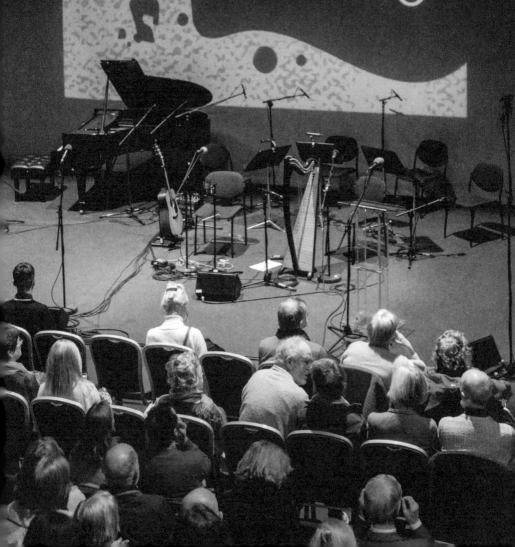

INTRODUCTION

Miscellany50 began as an idea to celebrate the fiftieth year of *Sunday Miscellany*. Broadcasting on RTÉ Radio since 1968, *Sunday Miscellany* is Ireland's longest-running weekly programme, featuring short essays and, occasionally, poetry with music and song interspersing the spoken contributions. It is only fitting, in wanting to celebrate the much-loved *Miscellany*, to turn to the written word to capture its essence – partly out of nostalgia and partly out of homage. The result was *Miscellany50*, the radio festival weekend, and subsequently, this eponymous anthology.

As I write my introduction, I have beside me the nine previous *Sunday Miscellany* anthologies edited variously by Ronnie Walshe, Marie Heaney and myself. They are somewhat mauled now from much handling over the years from their use as a working reference for the programme.

The volumes also serve as testimonies to the *Sunday Miscellany* phenomenon, described in an introduction to one of these anthologies as 'honouring the essence of its first broadcast when it went out on air in 1968, promoted in the *RTÉ Guide* as part of a brand-new strand of programming designed to have "greater listener involvement" and "appeal to listeners of all ages"'.

Indeed, along the years, others not directly associated with the programme have noted its 'bringing together known and lesser-known writers in a celebration of the rich fabric of life and culture, the inventiveness of the human voice and the scope of the mind' and as being 'in the most flattering sense, a very strange and radical little radio show'. There was even a call for the programme 'to be declared a national institution [as it] oscillates between travellers' tales [. . .] parish histories, the place of poignancy in our lives, little mysteries of the everyday'.

In a classic *Sunday Miscellany* musing, a listener (and subsequently a reader) is transported through a taut piece of writing into another time and place, when the poet Austin Clarke recalled how he came to know from James Joyce which two Dublin streets Joyce preferred. Clarke spent a couple of months in Paris as a young man. Once a week he and Joyce met in a little street behind Saint-Sulpice to drink a few Pernod Fils. He remembers how

> Joyce was dejected at that time because the editor and print-ers of the American literary periodical *The Little Review*, in which extracts of *Ulysses* had appeared, were being charged with obscenity. He sat at the café table, gazing abstractly through his dim, glaucous spectacles, sighing to himself and sometimes asking me about some shop or street or pub . . . in Dublin. Once he brightened up for a few moments and said: 'Dublin is the nearest city to the continent. Places in Paris are like Capel Street and like Thomas Street on a Saturday night when people are bargaining for the Sunday dinner, the very faces I seem to see are the same' and then he sighed again.

Clarke then recalls how he wished he had told Joyce 'all [I] knew about those two streets for he might have used some of it in his great prose epic'. The poet at least shared much of his own associations with the two Dublin streets with *Sunday Miscellany* listeners:

> My mother had been born at No. 1 Thomas Street, and every month my sister and I hurried up Watkin Street to buy a stone of salt for the big salt cellar at home. We went by the dark form of St Catherine's Protestant Church which my mother had passed as fearfully when she was a youngster going on messages down to Castle Street.

Clarke's essay describes how he and his sister Cathleen once stole down Capel Street to a fruit shop on Ormonde Quay and hurried forward to see a red-coated regiment marching down from the barracks near Kingsbridge and the Infirmary Road. Suddenly we heard the clatter of hooves and knew at once that the Lord Lieutenant of Ireland and his escort were coming. We were just on time to see the lesser might of the British Empire pass by on that sunny afternoon, the Earl Dudley in his carriage and all his outriders and pistoleers. I would like to think that the exact date was 16 June 1904 for in *Ulysses* the Lord Lieutenant and his company came down by Ormonde Quay on that day.

I mention this by way of illustrating the breadth of the first-hand memory mined by contributors to *Sunday Miscellany* – the earliest stretching back to the turn of the twentieth century, just as the current crop of contributors are easing into our twenty-first century. All in fifty years of radio. Well worth celebrating.

And so, true to its subtle but continuous re-invention, *Miscellany50* became a sort of artist in residence at the Project Arts Centre in Dublin for a sell-out weekend of concerts at the end of 2018. The writing anthologised here was read there for the first time alongside a feast of music and song, the latter such rich material for another project, another day.

Fifty new essays and poems were commissioned by myself along with RTÉ music producer and presenter Aoife Nic Chormaic and Sarah Binchy, *Sunday Miscellany's* current producer. Writers were given one of fifty years since 1968 as their starting point. We commissioned a further five essays to set the scene to each new decade in the lifetime of the programme.

John Bowman (I: 1968–1977) establishes *Sunday Miscellany's* beginnings against the backdrop of the adrenaline-fuelled birth of Irish television, which by the end of the 1960s led to the shaping of radio into the media form it is today.

Mary O'Malley (II: 1978–1987) casts the distant but clear eye of an emigrant. She read in letters about the visit of Pope John Paul II and the volatile tensions of contemporary politics; when the hunger strikes made international news; and when Ronald Reagan came to town. And as the so-called brain drain of the middle classes took off, people began to sit up and notice that the country was once more haemorrhaging from mass emigration. At the same time she recalls there was lobbying for peace and divorce and social justice – not, at the time, subjects discussed on *Sunday Miscellany*.

Joseph O'Connor (III: 1988–1997) also spent years abroad, reminding us how common a feature the boat was between Holyhead and Dún Laoghaire. He supposes everyone has their own London 'made of images and memories as much as places', and explains how coming and going between Ireland and London created a disjointedness, a sense of belonging in neither one place nor another. But with the election of Mary Robinson the gradual changes that were afoot became tangible and, as he puts it, 'impossible things were happening'. They would lead to the Good Friday Agreement and a new hopefulness, which also brought him back home for good.

Colin Murphy (IV: 1998–2007) graduated from college into the Celtic Tiger. The boom was booming. People were coming home. His account of movement through the decade was fuelled by a personal quest rather than out of economic necessity. He went 'the other way' – to Spain, Angola, South Africa. Rather than being a judgement on the general possibilities of new-found wealth, Murphy's essay is a reminder that amidst public expectations to conform, our interior world requires space to breathe. In time, love brought Murphy back to Ireland; becoming a parent made his house a home.

Lisa McInerney (V: 2008–2017) picks up on the cusp of when the crash happened, when she started 'writing short, sarcastic pieces online about the state of the place'. Hers is the most immediately familiar content, being so close to the present and with references to 'redundancies and pay cuts' and of being 'too broke to emigrate, and too sure of what was coming to try to head it off'.

But aptly, in the context of *Sunday Miscellany*, McInerney goes on to reflect on how the current writing boom may be propelled by our constantly changing landscape, circumstances and environment; how so much, from water charges and the right to a home, to equality and migration, has been contested in the past decade.

These five essays reflect the personality of their authors and were written independently of what the subsequent writers in each decade sing or shout about, lament or question. Together they offer an imaginative scaffolding on which to hang the other fifty essays of this anthology.

Mirroring the regular *Sunday Miscellany* way of gathering material for the weekly radio programme, some of the *Miscellany50* writing was selected from an open submission call. The rest was commissioned, from both long-time contributors to the programme as well as writers new to the enterprise. There are contributions in Irish (with specially translated versions for this book into English by their authors) and in English, as has also been the case with *Sunday Miscellany* since 1968.

While it is obvious from a 2019 vantage point that *Sunday Miscellany* started out as something of an exclusive gentleman's club (as referenced by John Bowman), that male bubble was sporadically punctured by a maverick female voice – think Nuala O'Faoláin, Hilary Boyle, Maeve Binchy, Hilda Murphy, Val Mulkerns and so on. These contributions rarely made it into the early *Sunday Miscellany* anthologies of writing, although things did improve along the years and the variety in this anthology illustrates the diversity of voices the programme draws in today

Take, for example, the essays that bookend *Miscellany50*. In the opening piece, set in 1968, a young bride-to-be fusses over her bouquet on the morning of her wedding. In the final essay, set more or less fifty years later, a first-time mother pushes her pram in the wake of Storm Ophelia. For Mae Leonard the fussing over flowers and her waiting taxi are what she puts to work to capture the love between a father and daughter. For Jessica Traynor a storm is the backdrop for a meditation on the joys and anxieties of first-time motherhood.

Between these two short essays stretch five decades, but then that is only accounting for literal years. There are actually multiples of whole lives and experiences in the mix. They reveal the mind at a profoundly personal and considered level of thinking alongside more objectively factual or humorous takes on what animates, engages or provokes the contributors to articulate and share.

What is exhilarating but obvious when you think about it is that, as Gemma Tipton, says, 'there are always more than two sides to everything' – and more than two ways of seeing and experiencing things. The ordinary, the particular to each of us, is elevated through the transaction that happens between the imagination of an open, curious writer and an engaged listener – and now, reader.

As another anthology is published, *Sunday Miscellany*'s signature tune, the inimitable brassy sound of Samuel Scheidt's 'Galliard Battaglia', continues to introduce the programme every Sunday morning. Saluting fifty years, this book is dedicated to all its contributors, makers, and most importantly *Sunday Miscellany*'s past, present and future listeners who ultimately ensure the show goes on.

Clíodhna Ní Anluain
Executive Producer and Editor, *Miscellany50*
September 2019

I
1968-1977

SETTING THE SCENE

John Bowman

I can remember the old Radió Éireann in the 1960s. It had yet to evolve and be branded to become today's RTÉ Radio 1.

In 1961 broadcasting in Ireland was being transformed. It was a time of innovation, creativity, and risk-taking. But, initially, this was all happening on a greenfield site in Donnybrook where the new television studios were being built. Meanwhile in the GPO the old Radió Éireann felt marginalised and was finding it difficult to adapt to the new climate.

And it was not much helped by a brash young Bostonian director-general, Edward J. Roth, whose broadcasting experience was in television and whose preoccupation was to ensure that the new television service would be on air by the end of 1961. It launched on New Year's Eve. Roth was not much in evidence in the radio station and he did not endear himself to staff when one of his first decisions was to take all women newsreaders off the air – as it was his belief that they 'lacked authority' when reading the news.

Radio also lost some of its leading young broadcasters, individuals of the calibre of James Plunkett, Gerard Victory, Maeve Conway, Michael Garvey and John O'Donoghue, all of whom had left the GPO to take up careers in the new television service. In the early 1960s the focus was on television; radio had not anticipated these changes and had neglected the potential of daytime radio broadcasting.

It took Radió Éireann some years to get its act together. But radio did begin to assert itself just fifty years ago in the late 1960s. It would have to develop formats which were best suited to radio: including access to the airwaves by listeners who telephoned to give live personal testimony to a national audience on any number of subjects – many of them previously taboo. And, ironically, it was the brash new television service which had first debated these topics. Indeed, so absent were they on Radió Éireann before the television breakthrough that so far as current affairs were concerned it could be called the golden age of *silent* radio.

But once television had become embedded the radio service took stock. It discovered that daytime broadcasting provided a challenge. And it quickly appreciated that women especially could contribute through radio in a sort of early version of what I might call 'me too' testimony. Any number of individual case histories could make compelling radio and embolden other women to recognise that they had shared some of the same experiences. Cumulatively, these debates challenged policies that particularly affected women's lives and which had hitherto been determined by men – bishops, doctors, lawyers and politicians.

This point is well illustrated by taking one issue central to women that was transformed in the 1970s: policy on family planning and specifically on the availability of contraceptives. Within a decade the question asked in broadcast debates moved from: 'Is it a sin?' to 'Why is it a crime?' to 'Is it not a civil right?' Such an historic and rapid shift in public attitudes left the old guard – the bishops, doctors, lawyers and politicians – somewhat stranded.

Along with opening up such debates radio at this period also expanded its news and current affairs coverage. That this coincided with the beginnings of the Northern Ireland Troubles provided further challenges. And the situation in the North quickly deteriorated: there were 16 deaths in 1969; 24 in 1970; and 170 in 1971. The death toll peaked at 472 in 1972 and there were some 1200 in the following five years.

All of this meant that the radio schedule fifty years ago was unrecognisable from that of just a decade earlier. But one of the new programmes did carry some of the old values. This was *Sunday Miscellany*. It could have originated in what were once known as the Talks Departments in many public service radio stations. BBC's Lord Reith, who established this tradition, would have approved.

It was scarcely groundbreaking. Rather, it was the successful melding of two ingredients: ideas and music. And it allowed listeners to do some of the work themselves. I was reminded of the great Francis MacManus, Head of Features in Radió Éireann, who liked to quote the small boy who preferred radio to television because, as he said, 'the pictures were better on radio'.

Sunday Miscellany was considered reflective and especially well suited to Sunday morning listening. The poet Emily Dickinson might have considered that it was a good way to 'keep the Sabbath'. But who would have thought in 1968 that the programme would still be around fifty years later? Probably not the schedulers. They were pencilling in a reliable format, well within the competence of those in charge.

And to whom is the credit due for the historic success of the programme? Well, to the successive producers of course; and to the writers whose talks proved so interesting to so many; and to the heads of department who continued to recognise a success; and to the musicians playing the music as chosen and to the composers of that music. *Sunday Miscellany* has always had an eclectic choice of music; and it knew only two kinds, good and bad.

But I would venture that most of the credit is due to you, the listeners. You are the people who appreciate *Sunday Miscellany* in such numbers that it has not only survived but gone from strength to strength. Today, it is highly popular with listeners in Ireland and also with listeners around the world, who podcast the show, or hear it online.

I will end by risking a paraphrase of Emily Dickinson:

> Some keep the Sabbath going to church –
> I keep it, staying at home –
> With a radio-set for a chorister –
> And talk and music for a Dome –
>
> On *Sunday Miscellany* remember
> the sermon is never long,
> so instead of getting to Heaven, at last –
> I'm going, all along.

RTE GUIDE

PROGRAMMES NOVEMBER 30–DECEMBER 6 :: Vol. 11 No. 48 :: IRIS RADIO TELEFIS EIREANN, NOVEMBER 29, 1974.   PRICE 5p.

Ronnie Walsh presents Sunday Miscellany RTE RADIO

Historian Maurice Craig (left) and men of letters Anthony Cronin and John Jordan . . . among the Sunday Miscellany ' regulars '. Benedict Kiely (left) and Stephen Rynne . . . contributing to the series.

"SUNDAY MISCELLANY": Radio: Sunday.

YOUR SUNDAY SOUFFLÉ

HAS ANYONE ever explained what Debussy found so evocative about Sabbath morning at sea that he should write a piece of music about it? Some shipping companies are known to dish out a Sunday lot of men to the crew and beer to the officers (which is a peculiar distinction in itself). Otherwise, the Sabbath morning at sea might as easily be Wednesday, or Monday.

Maybe Debussy was thinking of a ship plying close to shore, with, in the distance, a glimpsed church steeple, and from that steeple the sound of bells coming faintly to the mariners' ears. Or, if he had lived longer and listened to RTE on the ship's radio, he might have been thinking of *Sunday Miscellany*, which in its six years of service has come to evoke for many of us the very essence of Sunday morning.

The studio at Donnybrook where *Miscellany* is put together has about it on Tuesday afternoons something of the air of a country kitchen. When I arrived, John Jordan was talking with evident enjoyment about noses and Laurence Sterne, and Ronnie Walsh was smiling appreciatively. John Ryan dropped in to discuss a bizarre topic with Ronnie. It sounded like it might be about the weather — rain was mentioned a lot, and also polar ice-caps.

"Dia 'sa teach. Did you get my message?" Benedict Kiely entered, searched his person for a script, grinned at Anthony Cronin, who was reading a thoughtful piece on Milton in the sound-proof caboosh. "Excellent, Antóin," said Ben when he emerged. "I couldn't have done it better meself."

In between, Ronnie Walsh managed to talk about the programme. The apparently casual approach emphasises rather than conceals the fact that it is the work of a set of highly professional broadcasters. Most ideas for topics come from the contributors, normally shaped by talk among themselves and with him. He must contrive that the range of subjects and choice of music ("one of the most difficult jobs") will give a distinctive flavour to each programme.

"I like the analogy of an imaginative omelette." Stew? "Well . . . perhaps a soufflé."

There are no real precedents for *Sunday Miscellany*. J. B. Priestley's talks, Alistair Cooke — not quite the same sort of thing. Producer Cathal Ó Gríofa recalls they thought of including scientific talks from the BBC, perhaps some scenes from plays. In the event, the format emerged as it is today. Both Cathal and Ronnie Walsh stress their luck in having available a number of writers who were also excellent radio performers. Eric Cross, Stephen Rynne, Hilary Boyle, Dominic Roche, Gerard Kane, both now dead; the list of talent could fill a paragraph. They made possible that most pleasing characteristic, that every piece is read by its creator. Avoiding the twin perils of pedantry and sentimentality, a graceful blend of drollery and erudition has made of *Sunday Miscellany* a unique form of radio entertainment. May we call it our university of the air?

John Walsh

Hilary Boyle . . . featured in the Sunday morning radio programme.

Presenter Ronnie Walsh and producer Cathal Ó Gríofa . . . lucky in having writers available who were also excellent radio performers.

6 August 1968

Mae Leonard

It is 6 August 1968 and I'm all dressed up and ready to go. The taxi is waiting. Well-wishers have gathered outside the front door. But my father is missing. I hear some rattling noises coming from upstairs. and I call him. 'Dad! Dad!'

No answer.

And I pause and smile remembering him reading the opening lines of *Tom Sawyer* to us at bedtime: '*TOM!*' *No answer.* '*What's gone with that boy, I wonder? You TOM!*' *No answer.*

That flash of nostalgia has tears welling in my eyes.

And then I hear my father's voice as he comes down the stairs. 'She found it,' he mutters.

'Dad. The taxi's outside. It's time to go.'

But he's not listening. He's pulling books from the bookcase and they're slapping onto the floor.

'Dad! We'll be late.'

'Your mother must have found it.'

'Found what?'

No answer.

Now he is crawling under the sideboard. I don't need this right now.

Things have been bad enough all morning – starting with the flowers. Roses. I wanted lily of the valley or freesia but they're out of season. So, it was Hobson's choice. Take it or leave it. Roses. A friend – the head gardener at the People's Park in Limerick – promised that he'd have my flowers ready. My brother drove me there early just as the staff were being given instructions for the day, but there was no sign of my friend. 'He's on holidays,' I was informed and I stood there in shock horror with tears about to run down my face. 'But . . . but . . . but he was supposed to have my flowers ready.'

One look at my face and his second in command grabbed secateurs, told me to wait and returned with a dozen of the most magnificent long-stemmed roses. But how do you make a posy with those? Back at home my brother's wife stepped into the breach and managed to make them look elegant by tying three together with white satin ribbon. But I really wanted lily of the valley or freesias.

The clock chimes eleven.

'Dad! We have to go.'

He scrambles out from under the sideboard and is covered in dust and cobwebs.

'Ha! Your mother didn't find this one,' he says, triumphantly holding up a flat bottle. He unscrews the cap.

'Dad, you can't go to church smelling of whiskey.'

'I need a drop of Dutch courage,' he says, smacking his lips, and then he pauses and offers me the bottle. I shake my head and he takes another swig. And as he screws the cap back on, I catch a glimpse of myself in the sideboard mirror. I stoop to check my hair. Yes, at least that looks good. My hairdresser did me proud. There's cluster of curls at the back of my head with a scattering of white flowers pinned around them.

But my dress?

'Dare to be different,' my best friend said. 'Knit your dress.' We were big into knitting at the time. I really wanted the stunning shower-of-hail dress displayed in Gibson's Ladies' Fashion House uptown. But I allowed myself to be convinced to knit my dress. My mother was denied the frills and flounces and lace and the Limerick lace veil she expected me to choose.

A work colleague found a suitable design in a women's magazine that wasn't too difficult a pattern to knit. The yarn had to be ordered specially by the craft department in Cannock's. It was glistening white with a satin thread running through it. My mother shook her head and refused to have hand act or part in it. My friends and workmates assisted in every way they could – working out the instructions of the pattern, measuring and blocking out all the bits, stitching the seam – and you know what? It turned out quite lovely. It is a two-piece suit in a lacy pattern – a short skirt and top that comes halfway down over it.

And now the sideboard mirror tells me it's – well, definitely different.

I turn around to brush the dust and cobwebs off Dad's new suit.

'Do I look all right now?' he asks as he pockets the whiskey bottle. I pause. It's the look in his eyes that makes me catch my breath. He's going to say something like 'I'll miss you' but words would be an intrusion. That look is enough. Tears are very close. I have to look away but I manage to say, 'You're a right handsome fella.'

A very demanding beep from the taxi shatters the moment.

I ease on my white crochet gloves, finger by finger, and I pick up my roses. Someone takes a photograph of himself and myself, arms linked, making our way up the aisle. There's the outline of a whiskey bottle in his right-hand pocket and the clock on the gallery behind us is showing eleven twenty.

The rest of our wedding day ran so smoothly it's a blur to me except for one little moment – when we arrived at the Shannon Arms Hotel for our reception I was accosted by a flustered waitress – 'Have you seen the bride, love, we can't serve the champagne until she arrives.' So much for daring to be different and knitting my wedding dress.

One Small Step in Journalism

John Boland

It was the year of *Easy Rider*, which assured us that, even with dreary old Dev still up in the Park, we were all born to be wild. Such an unmissable movie then, and so unwatchable now. Great soundtrack, though.

It was the year of Woodstock and all of its feel-good vibes about peace and love, and a few months later of the Altamont Festival, too, where Hells Angels stabbed a guy to death in front of the stage and all the love curdled.

It was the year in which the British army arrived in the North, Charles Haughey announced tax exemptions for artists and Samuel Beckett won the Nobel Prize, causing his wife Suzanne to exclaim, '*Quelle catastrophe!*'

And it was the year when Neil Armstrong took his one small step onto the Moon, and when yours truly took an even smaller step into journalism, a profession he had never considered while sitting for his final arts degree exams in Earlsfort Terrace.

But that had been six months earlier and my father, plainly concerned at my aimless mooching around the house, finally wondered whether, given my interest in writers, I had ever thought of a career in journalism. As it happened, he knew just the man to contact in the *Irish Press*, so if I was at all interested, he'd make a phone call.

And thus I ended up being interviewed by the paper's managing editor, W.J. Redmond, a large Dickensian character with fearsomely bushy eyebrows, who scanned my paltry CV, observed that I'd published some poems and a few prose pieces in the UCD literary magazine *St Stephen's* and drily declared that he couldn't give a hoot if I'd written *Ulysses* so long as I was up to the job in hand.

That job initially involved a stint as the newsroom's diary clerk, which meant that I was obliged to note down in a huge ledger details of forthcoming court cases, Dáil debates, county council meetings, sporting fixtures, concerts and numerous other sundry events. It wasn't exactly challenging work, yet such was the charged atmosphere all around me as reporters rushed to meet deadlines for the evening paper's three editions that within a month I never wanted to be anywhere else than among these fascinating and pos- sibly unhinged people in pursuit of their stories.

There was nothing unhinged, though, about Michael Mills, the morning paper's political correspondent and later Ireland's first ombudsman, whose kindly gravitas made him an early mentor as he advised me on the best current American novelists to read – Updike and Mailer being special favourites of his.

And there were other mentors too, notably David Marcus, who edited the morning paper's New Irish Writing page and whose assistant I was fortunate to become for a year or so; and Con Hou- lihan, whom I encountered in the Pearl Bar on the night of an All-Ireland final and who, with nowhere to stay, ended up in the Pembroke Road flat I shared with my girlfriend, where he resided for nine months, during which time I learned a lot about life, liter- ature and the interiors of public houses.

Of the latter, the favourites among press people were Mulli- gan's of Poolbeg Street (known as the branch office) and the Scotch House and Silver Swan on Burgh Quay, the latter familiar to all of us as the Mucky Duck and now long gone.

So, too, are many of the *Press* colleagues who so enlivened my early newspaper years. It's become a truism among older journalists – many of whom went on to *The Irish Times*, the *Irish Independent* and RTÉ – that the *Press* was both a brilliant training ground and a fun place in which to work, but it really was.

In all my time there, I never encountered any of the bullying that I've detected in some other media institutions or any of the routine misogyny, either – it may not have promoted many women to executive positions (few newspapers did then) but it never countenanced the notion that they were less than equal to their male colleagues. And its insistence on factual accuracy was so drilled into its journalists that it incurred few successful libel actions.

I left after eight years – during which time I had been subeditor, reporter, feature writer, theatre and film critic and book reviewer – to become arts editor of the weekly *Hibernia*, with John Mulcahy, who passed away this year, as my civilised and kindly boss. That was an enriching experience, too, but when *Hibernia* folded after three years I returned to the comforting embrace of the *Press* until it, too, folded in 1995. Maybe it was all too comforting, and certainly in an era when mendacious Twitter campaigns and cries of fake news have led to serious journalism around the world becoming increasingly embattled, institutions like the *Press* seem to belong to a vanished age when newspapers actually meant something.

Mother Moon

Nuala O'Connor

Mother Moon sails above the Earth by night, watching over us, lighting our way with her glow that oscillates between salt glare and country-butter yellow. She is our Moon, the Moon, a seductive satellite, the night lantern we all find easy to love. And like many things that arouse passion, people have long wanted to possess the Moon: to peer at her up close, to touch her unknown skin, to examine her crannies and get to know her intimately. To take things from her. And so we have built machines and flown up to meet her, to explore her surface and record her dimensions; to conquer her.

Only a dozen people have managed to walk the Moon's land, to take measure of her as a farmer might a new field. And the twelve apostles of the Moon were all, of course, men: Buzz Aldrin, Neil Armstrong, Alan Bean, Gene Cernan, Pete Conrad, Moss Duke, James Irwin, Stuart Roosa, Jack Schmidt, Dave Scotts, Al Shepard and Jim Young. No woman has yet planted her foot on the lunar mantel, or had the opportunity to talk about giant, inclusive leaps for all of humankind.

Apollo 11 was the first spaceflight to succeed in landing men on the Moon. Americans Neil Armstrong and Buzz Aldrin landed their lunar module, *Eagle*, in July 1969, and Armstrong was the first human to step onto the lunar surface. The pair spent over two hours collecting more than twenty kilos of Moon rock to bring back to Earth. What joy they must have felt to look at, lift, and carry this alien material, these sandy, piddocked rocks that would tell them so much about the make-up of Mother Moon.

Apollo 12 was a success too, the spacecraft landed on the Moon's Ocean of Storms. Mission 12 brought the first colour TV camera to the Moon, but in a true Mr Bean moment, lunar-module pilot Alan Bean destroyed the camera by pointing it at the sun.

As for the following Apollo mission, one wonders if 13, that trickiest of numbers, was the best digit to give the foray that left Earth in April 1970, to once again try to possess the Moon. Might the powers-that-be not have jumped a number, for security's sake? For suspicion's?

Mission 13, famously, would be both failure and success. Apollo 13's task was to land on the Moon's Fra Mauro formation, an area of hills, ridges and possible moonquake debris, that was believed to hold important clues to the Moon's geological make-up. Two days into the flight, an oxygen tank ruptured on board, causing serious damage but, miraculously, though they couldn't land on the Moon as planned, none of the crew was injured or killed.

Astronaut Jack Swigert uttered the iconic, but latterly botched, Houston line. He actually said, 'OK, Houston, we've had a problem here' and this phrase was repeated by his colleague Jim Lovell as, 'Uh, Houston, we've had a problem.' For drama, in the 1995 film about the mission, the phrase was altered to the present tense and that's the one that's remained in the popular consciousness.

Once Apollo's in-flight disaster happened, the three astronauts' training kicked in, in tandem with the skills of those at control in Houston, and the slow-moving drama of getting the men back to Earth began. It played out over four days, but astronaut Fred Haise said he never felt their situation was hopeless and neither did his colleagues. Mother Moon was smiling her benevolence on them for sure. Astronaut Jim Lovell said about his experiences:

> The lunar flights give you a correct perception of our existence. You look back at Earth from the Moon, and you can put your thumb up to the window and hide the Earth behind your thumb. Everything you've ever known is behind your thumb, and that blue-and-white ball is orbiting a rather normal star, tucked away on the outer edge of a galaxy.

In the mid-1800s poet Emily Dickinson asked a friend in a letter, 'Do you look out to-night? The moon rides like a girl through a topaz town.' The Moon remains our fair girl, backdropped with topaz; she is a rolling pearl across an ink bowl; a ball of plaster of Paris; she is a milk-glass plate that is resolutely ours, just as our own planet is; she is a normal star in an extraordinary galaxy. And she is a comforting beacon, our radiant night-mother. Our Moon.

Me and Bobby McGee

Leo Cullen

There was something about Charley McCartney with the strong Derry accent, something more than the easy-going demeanour, more than the flashing smile – the attractively broken tooth received from falling off a wall in Derry when running away from something . . . the army, the RUC, a girl, he never did say.

It had been a long time since I'd thought of Charley. Nietzsche, it was, who brought it on – the day last summer I descended from Èze, an ancient mountaintop village on the Côte d'Azur. The Mediterranean was shining up at me, the path was winding, dangerous and shaly and I was taking the same route Nietzsche the philosopher had once taken. Along the route I read plaques on which were printed snatches of his thoughts. His will to power. His philosophy on friendship.

But let's get back to Charley. 1971: Instead of hanging around after failing exams, I headed for America. Winter started early and snowy in New York. I was living in the Bronx with Carl Egan who worked on the buildings. Some days the heating boiled over in the house and we melted, some days it didn't come on and we froze. One day Charley walked in, though I don't remember why. He had a way of striking up a rapport. He knew how to get by; he had tips for dealing with bosses, unions, cops, the city. His outlook was more straightforward and his life more freewheeling than were our rites of passage. And when one day Carl and I boarded the D train on Fordham Road, got off somewhere in mid-Manhattan, ran until we landed in a sweat at the yoga house in Greenwich Village where we were to be initiated into transcendent meditation, Charley only laughed at us.

In early December he began talking of Trexler; he said we should meet this great character. Trexler lived in Denver. He skied the Colorado slopes, he stalked bear. We should chuck in our jobs and come with Charley to Denver. Man, it was cool in Colorado.

He persuaded me to go. I was leaving a promising job: window-cleaning on Fifth Avenue – clear prospects. Carl stayed at the cement work. On a wet Christmas Eve morning we stuck out our thumbs on the Jersey turnpike. Heavy trucks threw up sprays of road-surface water on our faces and clothes. Christmas Day passed us somewhere along the road. After Chicago the trouble began. Nobody would pick us up. For days we stood with our thumbs raised. I thought the truckers were out to get us. They'd lurch towards us in passing, blow hooters, we'd see fists through windscreens: 'Get lost, hippies!'

'Just give them the peace sign,' Charley said.

Then one evening, darkness coming down, a van pulled in and the driver, black guy, opened his window and said, 'Where you goin'?'

'Denver.'

'Come aboard.'

There were four of them, two black guys, two whites. Hopping about on top of the dashboard was a thick paperback. I asked what it was. 'Nietzsche,' the Afro-haired driver said, 'we never go anywhere without him.'

In the back of the van mattresses were strewn sleeping bags, music cassettes; a stove was lit to make us coffee. They were on a mission: carrying a stash of cannabis saved in summer fields somewhere down south; taking it to Seattle where they would sell it. They were doing other things too – avoiding the draft. And *whitey* America. Saying that, they laughed at the variety of their skin colours. They were unusual company, though maybe they found Charley more unusual than he did them. He told them they didn't need Nietzsche, hash or revolution but they'd be welcome to stay in his place in Derry whenever he'd get home.

One night our van trundled over the Mississippi. The Allman Brothers were playing on the cassette deck. Two mornings later, we hit Denver. We whizzed right through as supermarkets opened, Charley telling me we'd head on to Seattle and we could return to Denver another time to stalk bears with Trexler.

Our four dudes stopped now and then on the road but only to watch TV in diners – they told us that if you wanted to learn about America all you had to do was watch TV. One day a newsflash showed us Alabama segregationist governor George Wallace spewing racist hatred in his run for the 1972 presidency. Our hosts said, 'That's America. Somebody will shoot that guy.' Travelling onward, they read us *Thus Spoke Zarathustra*, gave lessons on Nietzsche's ideas on friendship. But according to Charley our resident oracle, Nietzsche – who he'd come across in Queen's University, Belfast – was not going to change what was happening anywhere, Ulster or Alabama.

In Reno the break-up occurred. On a basketball court in winter sunshine. Our Zarathustrans said, 'Let's stop, have a game,' so we did; three against three, Charley and I on opposing sides. Pitted against one another, we two began to fight; why ever I can't remember – maybe some long famine not until then allowed expression. Though I do remember the others egged us on: 'Look at the two little Irish guys – the fighting Irish.' It came to bitter words, heavy blows.

It was there in Reno that Charley took his rucksack from the van and slipped away. On a day I'll forever associate with frantic, wonderful, Janis Joplin and her rendition of 'Me and Bobby McGee': . . . *then somewhere near Salinas, Lord, I let him slip away* . . .

And so did I slip away. For the following year anyway; that year, 1972, somebody did shoot George Wallace. He lived. I never saw Charley again.

Charley, wherever you've found home, tell me why we fell out; tell me, were we friends in 1971? Maybe we were; friends as Nietzsche defined friends: friends are those who ask not the easiest ways of one another, not the least demanding ways; but the hardest ways, the most risk-worthy ways.

Always Remember, Never Forget

Denise Blake

I had a big birthday this year, one of those birthdays that makes you pause and think, 'How did this happen? Where has that time gone?' But birthday it was, so we had to celebrate.

It's funny how your perception of age alters as time progresses. I remember my grandmother saying, 'I still feel that I am a young woman.' And the teenage me was thinking, 'Nope. You're getting old, Granny.' But it is not that I mind getting older. My mother was forty-one when she died tragically, so then, years later, when I turned forty-two, it was a sudden gift, a freedom. I realised that each new year is one to treasure, no matter what age it adds up to.

So, for this big birthday we had a party on a warm Sunday afternoon. As people were gathering a friend of mine, Brenda, said to me, 'I need to show you something when you get the chance to look at it. I bet you'll want to write about this.'

When I did get the chance, I sat down beside Brenda and she opened her bag, took out an old school book, a geography book. Brenda had been at a neighbour's wake the day beforehand and the woman's daughter had given her this book. The daughter had used it in secondary school, but it had originally been Brenda's and had been owned by several different students during the seventies. Brenda placed the geography book in my hand. The front and back pages were covered with scrawled messages, all with the theme 'Always remember, never forget ...' I was bemused because I had been in a year behind Brenda in school. I didn't think this had anything to do with me personally.

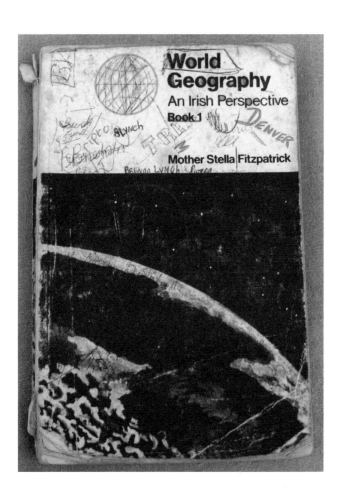

World Geography

An Irish Perspective

Book 1

Mother Stella Fitzpatrick

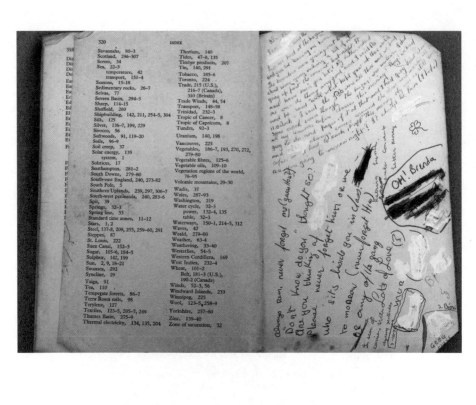

The geography book reminded me of a story from years ago when my son was in secondary school. He was sitting in English class, bored, as the teacher talked about *Hamlet*. A friend sitting beside him said, 'Look at the shape of my book, it is ancient, and there is all this mad writing through it.' My son said, 'Show me.' And to pass the time he started reading. He flicked through the pages and suddenly he saw my handwriting. *Always remember, never forget the day you saw M.G. walking up the town. Your cousin, Denise.*

And I laughed when he landed home from school and told me. That copy of *Hamlet* had first belonged to my cousin and had been passed on many times. Thankfully, I had written nothing incriminating on those pages. I don't know if she remembers who M.G. was, but I have no idea.

A friend of mine, who is a teacher, says students don't write messages like that anymore. *Always remember, never forget.* Nowadays books are hired or on loan and anyway, they use social media.

So here I was in my home, on my birthday, beside a friend, and with a memento of past times in my hands. I hadn't written in this particular book, but Brenda was anxious that I keep looking through the pages. I read through the inscriptions. *Always remember, never forget, it was in Loreto we first met.* The pages were covered in so many random messages and I knew the authors. *Never forget me – guess who. Remember your friend who sat beside you. Always remember today and you not having your homework done because you were at the bazaar. Never forget us in 2 Bróna. Are you going to the hop in the College tomorrow night?*

It was all there; dreaded classes, our head nun, the youth club, who got speaking to a college boarder, who was heartbroken, camogie games, parents, teachers and even the odd scored-out message after a break-up. Boys' names were written in code or just initialled, because of course, they never would be forgotten. Every word had been written secretly during a class or evening study hall.

Brenda was watching me carefully as I tried to decipher each piece of writing. And then, there tucked away amidst it all, in the smallest of handwriting, and without a signature, was the shortest message: *In memory of Denise's mother dying yesterday. 3/12/72.*

In that moment, my mother was back and with me in my living room.

Brenda smiled at me. She knew my mother, she knew what it was to see this message that was written when I was fourteen. To have this book, from her second year in the convent, that had been passed from Brenda to her younger sisters, to her neighbour's daughters, to be put away for years and then given back to Brenda again during a mother's wake and to be handed on to me the next day and on my sixtieth birthday.

And yes, as they all said so many years ago: *Always remember, never forget.*

Ó Chorcaigh, le Gean:
Miah, Seán agus Liam

Louis de Paor

Ar nós gach aon bhliain eile, is dócha, bliain mhór do Chorcaigh
ab ea 1973. Bhí Jimmy Barry-Murphy 19 mbliana d'aois is d'aim-
sigh sé dhá chúl nuair a bhuaileamar An Ghaillimh i gcluiche ceannais na hÉireann sa pheil. Bhí Frank O'Farrell ina bhainisteoir ar
Mhanchester United nó gur briseadh as a phost é go héagórach.
Tháinig Miah Dennehy isteach mar fhear ionaid nuair a d'imir An
Bhrasaíl, curaí an domhain, in aghaidh foireann uile-Éireann a bhí
tabhartha le chéile go neamhoifigiúil ag Johnny Giles agus Derek
Dougan. Protastúnach as Béal Feirste a d'imir le Wolverhampton
Wanderers ab ea Dougan, fear cruaidh neamhspleách a throid go
láidir ar son chearta a chomhimreoirí i Sasana. Bhí Jairzinho agus
Rivellino, ar fhoireann na Brasaíle an lá san ar Bhóthar Lansdún, Pat
Jennings agus Martin O'Neill, Giles agus Don Givens ar fhoireann
na hÉireann.

Agus Miah Dennehy as Corcaigh, ar ndóigh, an chéad duine
riamh a d'aimsigh trí chúl i gcluiche ceannais an FAI nuair a bhuail
Cork Hibernians Waterford United i 1972. Is cuimhin liom fós an
líonrith a bhí orainn á leanúint timpeall Perks Amusement Arcade in
Aird Mhóir, na sceitimíní áthais a bhí orm nuair a thoiligh m'athair
dul chuige i dtigh tábhairne Rooney chun a shíniú a fháil dom. Bhí
a fhios againn ná féadfadh aon rath a bheith ar Phoblacht na hÉireann nuair nár roghnaíodh Miah ach aon uair déag ar an bhfoire-
ann náisiúnta. Éire, ar ndóigh, a bhí thíos i gcónaí le haon ní a bhí
frith-Chorcaigh.

Sa bhliain 1973 d'fhágas-sa an bhunscoil is d'imigh Éamon de Valera ó Áras an Uachtaráin. Chuamar isteach san EEC is chuir rialtas na hÉireann deireadh le riachtanas na Gaeilge sa chóras oide-achais agus sa tseirbhís phoiblí. Ina cholún san *Irish Times,* d'fhógair an file Seán Ó Ríordáin go raibh ré na bhfear gaimbín tagtha, ré an neamhdhuine sa pholaitíocht. An té nár thuig gurbh é príomhbhua an pholaiteora a bheith ábalta dul siar ar a fhocal, ní raibh aon ghnó aige feasta i saol polaiticiúil na hÉireann, dar leis. Murab ionann le fealsaimh an Éithigh Nua ó dheas a chuir milleán na fola ó thuaidh ar an nGaeilge agus an Angelus, bhí fírinne neamhbhalbh, ar seisean, i bhfocail Ian Paisley agus Bernadette Devlin. Ba gheall le leanaí iad, adúirt sé, a bhíonn a rá rudaí drochbhéasacha.

Maidir leis an athchóiriú a bhí molta ar mhúineadh na staire ar scoil, d'fhógair sé nach uirlis ag rialtas ar bith an stair ach oiread leis an eolaíocht. Munar féidir linn ár slí a dhéanamh gan an fhírinne a mhaolú, tá ár bport seinnte, ar seisean. Murab ionann leis na polaiteoirí nár thug aon fhocal misnigh do mhuintir an tuaiscirt, adúirt sé, bhí Coslett Ó Cuinn, scoláire Gaeilge agus eaglaiseach Phro-tastúnach ó chathair Dhoire, ar a dhícheall á mhíniú do dhaoine go raibh an Ghaeilge fite fuaite le stair agus dúchas na bProtastúnach ó thuaidh.

Sibhialtacht agus aigne fé leith ab ea an Ghaeilge, de réir an Ríordánaigh, ionad faire neamhspleách agus cosaint riachtanach in aghaidh impiriúlachais an aonchultúir is an mhargaidh a bhí á chraobhscaoileadh ag lucht na cumhachta i mBaile Átha Cliath agus sa Bhruiséil. Ainneoin an drochmheas a bhí á chaitheamh ar oidhreacht na Gaeilge, bhí comharthaí ann, dar leis, go raibh sibhialtacht nua-aimsireach Ghaeilge á criostalú i measc na scríbh-neoirí óga a raibh saothar leo san iris fhilíochta *Innti.* Bhí suas le míle duine i láthair le haghaidh oíche mhór filíochta, ceoil, agus óil nuair a seoladh *Innti* 3 sa Vienna Woods Hotel i gCorcaigh i mí Aibreáin 1973. Bhí Máirtín Ó Direáin ann agus Somhairle Mac Gill Eain, mórfhile Gaeilge na hAlban, chomh maith le Michael Davitt, Gabriel Rosenstock, agus Liam Ó Muirthile, a cailleadh go hanabaí i mí Bealtaine na bliana so.

Eisiomláir ab ea Ó Muirthile den sibhialtacht nua-aimsireach Ghaeilge a bhí á bunú go ciúin gan buíochas do lucht na cumhachta de réir an Ríordánaigh. Ar nós an dá Sheán – Ó Riada agus Ó Ríordáin – atá curtha i Reilig Ghobnatan i gCúil Aodha ina theannta, mhúin Liam Ó Muirthile dúinn conas an scoilt idir Béarla agus Gaeilge, Éire is an Eoraip, an chathair is an tuath, idir dhá thaobh na habhann ionainn féin, a thrasnú:

> Saolaíodh tusa idir dhá linn, a Liam,
> greim an dá bhruach agat
> ar *no man's langue* a shaothraigh tú
> le fuil agus allas do phinn
> gur aimsigh do stáitse sa ghabhal
> idir dhá shruth na habhann,
> droichead guagach déanta d'fhocail
> gur féidir a shiúl anois id theannta.

> Is linne feasta an chuid sin dínn fhéin
> a nochtaigh tú dúinn i bhfoirm bhéarsaí
> sarar chuais le searc na laoch don scoil
> mar a bhfuilimidne fós ag foghlaim port
> is léinn agus sibhse ag iompar cré is cloch:
> Ó Riada, Ó Ríordáin, Ó Muirthile,

Corcaigh.

From Cork, with Love: Miah, Seán and Liam

Louis de Paor

Like every other year, you might say, 1973 was a big year for Cork.
Jimmy Barry-Murphy was nineteen and scored two goals when we
beat Galway in the All-Ireland Football Final. Miah Dennehy came
on as a sub when Brazil played an All-Ireland soccer team brought
together by Johnny Giles and Derek Dougan, a Belfast Protestant
who played with Wolverhampton Wanderers and fought hard for
the rights of his fellow players in England. Pelé's comrades from
the 1970 World Cup, Jairzinho and Rivelino, were there that day in
Lansdowne Road. We had Pat Jennings and Martin O'Neill, Giles
and Don Givens.

And Miah Dennehy, from Cork, the first player ever to score a
hat-trick in a FAI Cup Final when Cork Hibernians beat Waterford
United in 1972. I remember the excitement as we followed him
through Perks Amusement Arcade in Ardmore, the delight when
my father said he'd go in to Rooney's pub after him to get me his
autograph. We knew it spelled trouble for the Republic of Ireland
when they only picked Miah eleven times on the national soccer
team. Ireland always lost when there was anti-Cork bias in the mix,
from Kinsale to Saipan.

In 1973 Éamon de Valera left Áras an Uachtaráin and I finished national school. We joined the EEC and the government
ended the Irish language requirement in state examinations and
the public service. In his column in *The Irish Times*, the poet Seán
Ó Ríordáin declared the era of the gombeen man had arrived.

Anyone who failed to understand that the principal attribute of a politician was the ability to renege on his word had no place in Irish politics now, he said. Unlike the philosophers of the 'New Deceit' in the South who blamed Irish and the Angelus for the bloodletting in the North, he said, there was a blunt truth in the words of Bernadette Devlin and Ian Paisley. They were 'like children who say rude things,' he said, 'the more truth there is in what the child says the more it upsets the parent'.

As for the revision that was planned for teaching history in Irish schools, 'History is not something to be manipulated by any government,' he said, 'any more than science is. If we can't proceed without toning down the truth, we're finished.' Unlike the politicians who gave no word of hope to people in the North, Ó Ríordáin argued that Coslett Quinn, a Gaelic scholar and Church of Ireland minister from Derry was doing his utmost to show that the Irish language was part of the history and inheritance of his own people north of the border.

Irish was an alternative intelligence, according to Ó Ríordáin, an independent vantage point and a necessary defence against the monocultural imperialism transmitted by those in power in Dublin and Brussels. For all the official disrespect for the language, Ó Ríordáin saw signs that a modern Irish language civilisation was beginning to clarify itself in the poetry journal *Innti*. Among the young poets who read their work to an audience of up to a thousand people at the launch of the third issue of the journal in the Vienna Woods Hotel in Cork in May 1973, Ó Ríordáin mentioned Liam Ó Muirthile (who died in May 2018). Ó Muirthile, he said, exemplified an alternative civilisation that was establishing itself quietly despite the opposition of those in power.

Like the two Seáns, Ó Riada and Ó Ríordáin, who lie close to him in St Gobnait's cemetery in Baile Mhúirne, Ó Muirthile taught us how to bridge the gap and heal the wound between Irish and English, Ireland and Europe, between the two sides of the river inside ourselves:

You were born between two rivers and times,
holding on to the banks of that *no man's langue*
you claimed with the blood and sweat of your pen
coming ashore in the fork between two streams
where you found your home, a shaky bridge
of words we walk with you and after you.

We have it now, that part of ourselves you showed us
in verse before you left with the best of our heroes
to enter that school where we're still learning to speak
and sing while you and they are under clay and rock:
Ó Riada, Ó Ríordáin, Ó Muirthile,

                                                    Cork.

Starting Off

Gerald Dawe

I have no idea if there was an abbey to which our street was the gateway. Abbeygate Street, lower and upper, ran almost from the Convent School through the centre of Shop Street and down the other side of the Four Corners, shouldering Lynch's Castle along the way. It was a busy spot even then and in our hidden-away flat known as The Archway, on the ground floor, we sat within the gardens, yards and lanes of the town's inner world. 1974 could have been 1964 and I suppose 1954 for all that.

Traffic was light enough in the mornings. Gulls had a right of way and the occasional dog ambling its way around before business started up and the trucks and trailers edged around the tight corners.

I wrote about what I imagined I could hear in that retreat. The sound of the Corrib cascading through the eel nets underneath the Salmon Weir Bridge. The steadily still movement of the canal water where an occasional salmon weaved back and forth and the tumult of the river itself in full spate hitting under the span of Wolfe Tone and O'Brien Bridges, before spreading out into the Claddagh Basin and the eventual sea.

Galway seemed to have issued out of water. The lough, the river, the canals, the bay, the Atlantic. And all the other landing places had their own rowing clubs, piers, gates, weirs. Newtownsmith. Waterside. Woodquay. Some had little-known, out-of-the-way, sleepy spaces untroubled for ages, where houses, mills and granaries stood silently, often abandoned, in the shadow of the buoyant rhythm of river sounds. It was mesmeric.

I would sit in the city library above the courthouse and read the tales of William Carleton. Outrageously a swan settled itself along the riverbank. After a disturbance – a car horn bleated, or a dustbin lid clattered to the ground – the swan raised itself upon the tranquil waters and in seconds had taken off.

At other times the river was drained and away down on the riverbed you could make out the patterns of the Corrib's scything run over stone and gravel floor. It was a city of water like no other I had known. You could say that I had become water-borne. From my first glimpse of the endless distractions of the canal way on Nun's Island, to the dropping levels of the weir gate at Dominic Street and by the Long Walk, the opening skyline to the west altered the relation between the ground underfoot and the vastness beyond of the sea.

In the tiny back bedroom of the flat in Abbeygate Street I was like a refugee who had pitched up in what was my new place. There was a garden the size of a postage stamp and a formidable high brick wall. Next door the Roaring Twenties pub did a roaring trade. The shops out front – just large enough for a couple of people to stand in – like the folks who lived overhead, probably didn't know, that it all, soon, would begin to completely change.

The canal ways have now been opened up via a stunning parade skirting the River Corrib. You can follow its magnificent course from the marooned railway arches all the way to the sea and imagine, if you have a care to, the barges and boats and liners that reached around the globe to and from the heartland of Galway over the generations of emigrant and migrant; leaving and returning; finding a place.

I tried my hand at poem after poem in The Archway until something sounded half right. This short piece was written about that time we lived there, starting off, in 1974:

The Bells of St Nicholas

The bells of St Nicholas
reverberate through a fragile
morning, and over broken glass
the cat is poised to climb
the Post Office tower or wait
there for hours until you
call out her name.
So mornings were the same –
stretching to find the sky
lowered around this sleeping
city, the bells of St Nicholas
reach across bedsitting
rooms to the caravan camps,
and over rooftops of quiet hotels
a flight of gulls descends in tattered glory.

Old warehouses and merchant
houses as if ransacked
inside — buddleia spouts from
chimneys in narrow streets
that wind down to the sea.
On evening walks alongside
willowy canals the dog runs
ahead to the convent wall.
What did we say then,
under cover of night,
about my passage west
or your next trip home?
The swans coasted near,
untouchable and immune.

Kathmandu by Yellow Bus

Evelyn Conlon

An odd dangerous frisson happens before diving into the memory pool; people could break their necks if they accidentally hit the shallow end, which may have become so, not because little happened, but because you've deliberately cleared out that end and left only a shimmering, happily-dishonest mirage. But, here, let's risk it, let's dip.

In 1972 I went by ship to Australia, in 1975 I came back by bus.

The ship was a thing, but the bus, now the bus, that was another matter entirely.

I can still see the travel agent's window with the ad for the Sundowners Overland Tour, Kathmandu to London. Who could resist? Well as it turns out many people, and for good reason.

The journey began with a hop to Singapore from Sydney, a mere nine-hour flight, where travellers were met with notices portraying precise hair lengths considered suitable for men; barbers at the airport could insist on giving a trim to those not complying. In the post office a hairy man could be forced to the end of the queue, the signs clearly stating that 'Men With Long Hair Will Be Served Last', so you could technically spend forever getting a stamp. This attention to appearance did nothing to prepare us for arriving in Kathmandu, where the plane came in over the Himalayas, dropped from the sky like a hawk in a hurry, the pilot hitting the brakes, shuddering every bit of the machine and us, before we emerged into golden dust and a land where the men wore miniskirts.

On the morning that we assembled to board the yellow bus we were a cheerful lot, except those whose turn it was to be sick that day.

We peered at Vern, our Canadian guide, who had done this journey before and knew things we didn't about travelling through Asia and the Soviet Union. On an unairconditioned bus. Without the help of bottled water. If he had told us we wouldn't have believed him. From then on, diligently every night, he wrote out on a lined A4 notebook what we would see the following day. For the next three months, this grail, this prehistoric Google, was passed around and read avidly by us each morning, sometimes over one another's shoulders, such was the excitement. Before the camping month we stayed in cheap hotels, occasionally choosing slightly better, so we could wash clothes, have showers and drink perhaps less dangerous water. In no time at all we were in a world all of our own.

At Pokhara we saw the peaks of the Annapurna massif as we made the spectacular climb through the Himalayas, stopping occasionally in villages, always in search of a drink. Coca-Cola was the most available. Coming across roadside stalls we often drank a bottle in one mouthful. We couldn't imagine the invention of bottled water, and if we had done so it might have driven us mad.

All these years later, India can be summoned into one great cacophony of days out of a not-yet-written Rohinton Mistry novel. The Srinagar Lakes boatman who kept a pot of coal below his cape to keep himself warm comes to mind. As does the sight of our crock of a vehicle on the road from Pakistan to Afghanistan, chugging over the Hindu Kush mountains, through Landi Kotal, where, if you had the nerve to walk around the streets, we were told, you could buy smuggled anything from anywhere in the world. We took the Old Silk Road, crossed the Khyber Pass and the Kabul Gorge. We stopped and had tea with beautiful Afghani nomads in their tents, all of them wearing the most spectacular colours of red and blue, the men holding children in their arms, the women smiling at us strange, blanched people, the camels snorting and looking sideways out of their big eyes at the yellow bus. Years later I saw pictures of Herat being destroyed and remembered going to a theatre there, in a horse-drawn local taxi, the horse sporting red plumes, the hot night air full of music.

In Iran I remember roses and roses and roses. And the blue of Isfahan, where Omar Khayyam lived, and the sound of a street full of artisans chipping out designs on lamps, tables and all sorts of ornaments. Sometimes, when I get the chance to sit on a hot stone or wall, I remember Persepolis.

Four countries later we entered Ceauşescu's Romania, making our way to central Bucharest, in that year still called the Little Paris of the East. We saw the seven square kilometres of city that would soon be demolished to pander to his grandiose obsessiveness.

In a bookshop in Kishinev I looked for poems by Anna Akhmatova and Marina Tsvetaeva, cheeky enough now when I think about it. I didn't find them, but I bought the *Selected Works of Alexander Pushkin* in two volumes, one poetry, one prose. I still have them, with the price sticker intact.

Looking at that sticker last week I did indeed understand the danger of this memory diving, bearing in mind that danger has its good moments. The journey from Kathmandu to London took three months; we arrived an hour later than the advertised time.

It took me years to get on a bus. I still look at tours going past and say to anyone who will listen, 'Oh look, that bus has air conditioning.' But I will never forget the travel agent's window.

A Funny Thing Happened . . .

Denis Sexton

One bright October morning in 1976, I set out to change the world. Rather than jump into the car and drive to the school where I'd been teaching, I set off on foot for Bayside railway station. My wife waved me off. Though still hurting from having lost her own job thanks to the marriage bar, she was happy for me. At least she'd have the family car while I was away in training. Our three young children, however, were less pleased with the idea of Daddy being away so much. I could only hope that, despite the disruption to our family life, they, and perhaps their own children, might one day come to appreciate that Daddy's new job was worth the upheaval.

The aim was to replace the remnants of the old murder machine with a modern primary school curriculum. New pedagogic principles, new methodology, new furniture, new buildings, new relationships among the stakeholders, patrons, management, teachers, parents and pupils. And for the first time, formal recognition that some of our children do have special needs. As for the schools inspectorate, the challenge was to go out and preach this new gospel. If big ships are hard to turn around, the Irish education system would be as big as an ocean liner.

My wife decided that if I was going to be an inspector, I should look like one. So she bought me a trench coat. A long garment with impressive lapels and a storm flap. 'Aren't you confusing me with Inspector Clouseau?' I asked.

'Well, you don't want to look like an old-fashioned *cigire*, do you?' She was right. The *cigire* also needed a full makeover.

So, decked out in trench coat and carrying the shiny new *mála* supplied by the Department of Education, I arrived at Bayside station. Just in time to hear the tannoy: 'Howth train delayed.' No problem. I wasn't meeting my first mentor, Seán Mac Conmara, until ten o'clock. For two weeks I'd be with Seán for on-the-job training. Then off on similar postings around the country for six months. All going well, I'd finally get through *an triail* and be awarded my wings as a *cigire scoileanna*.

The tannoy crackled again. 'Indefinitely' came the word.

'It happens,' shrugged a veteran commuter. Yes, but what about me? My wife was taking the kids to school in the car and as for communication, nobody had yet bothered to invent the mobile phone. 'Howth Junction,' advised the veteran. 'Mainline train from there. Only half a mile along the track.' As he departed, he threw a word of comfort over his shoulder. 'And no fear of getting knocked down by a train.'

Half a mile. What was that to a man going off to change the world? Swinging my new *mála*, I stepped briskly from one wooden sleeper to another. The track was flat, a pleasant breeze blew in from Dublin Bay and the brass fittings on my *mála* gleamed in the morning sunshine. After about a hundred yards, things started to get awkward. Whoever had laid the sleepers had placed them too close together. For walking, they demanded the mincing gait of a high-heeled, tight-skirted woman. I tried skipping a sleeper; that resulted in my well-polished shoes plunging into the sharp flinty stones. Ignoring the pain, I soldiered on.

The 1971 new curriculum was possibly the most radical plan ever devised for Irish education. Change, however, didn't just linger in the air; two large brown-covered volumes contained full details of the plans for the new road ahead. I soon began to feel the weight of all this learning in more mundane quarters. With every step I took, my department *mála* thudded against my knee. Adding to the thud was a copy of the *Rules and Regulations for National Schools*, a note-book, various official circulars and of course the packed lunch my wife had made for her warrior.

As I stepped along the track I felt a medley of aches and pains spread from my knees to feet and shoulders and, as if to test me fully, the gentle breeze decided to morph into a gale. Roaring in over Bull Island, the wind whipped up the skirts and the lapels of my Clouseau trench coat. Like a flock of Furies they descended on me, flapping at my face, clawing at my eyes, tearing at my hair. Most vicious of all was the storm collar: I had fastened no more than a button or two, when it seemed as if the thing wanted to throttle me. Tugging and tearing at the collar, I reeled, staggered and stumbled along the track. Like Mad Sweeney, I howled at the elements; as I did, the wind roared back even louder.

Howth Junction, Kilbarrack, Connolly Station. Coming up Talbot Street I wondered why people were staring at me. My reflection in a shop window gave the answer: the storm collar. Hanging limply from my shoulder, it looked like a dead ferret. I tried to adjust it. No good. On the shoulder or off the shoulder, it continued to hang there like a very dead ferret. Glad to escape the gauntlet of shop windows, I turned into Marlborough Street. My via dolorosa was nearly at an end.

As I approached the Head Office of An Roinn Oideachais, the beggar sitting on the steps of the pro-cathedral lifted his head and gazed at me solemnly. Then, as if suddenly realising he had competition for his patch, he shouted across the road at me. In words that were less than prayerful, he urged me to keep moving. I limped through the black wrought-iron gates of the Department. Somewhere in the building I'd find a gents where I could make myself some way presentable.

As luck would have it, I met Seán Mac Conmara in a corridor. He was about to glance at his watch but when he saw the cut of the creature before him, his arm froze in mid-air. Silently he gaped at me. Never, since its foundation in 1831, had the schools inspectorate seen such an abject wretch dare to present himself as recruit material. In a daze, I clutched the briefcase. How could I explain to Seán? And my wife and kids waiting to hear about my day, what would I say to them when I got home?

It was then I noticed. They were winking, the brass fittings on my *mála* were winking up at me, as if to reassure me that despite the setbacks on the track for *mála* and me, the daring adventure of the 1970s reforms was only beginning.

I haven't read this piece to my older grandchildren. When it comes to Granddad's stories about the bad old days, they tend to get restless. Not so our latest granddaughter. Holding a wooden spoon and sitting in her highchair, Fiadh hung onto my every word.

'Well?' I asked.

She paused, then, like a hard Brexiteer applauding a speech by Boris, Fiadh banged, clattered and walloped her highchair with abandon.

I'll settle for that.

Jubilee Year

Gemma Tipton

You'll love it, my parents said. Maybe you can have a pony.
At nine years of age, this seemed like very heaven.
We moved to Ireland in 1977. In England it was the Queen's
Silver Jubilee: street parties and Union Jacks everywhere. People
revelling in the comfort of their Britishness.

In Ireland it was different. As a small and mainly smiling child,
I hadn't really experienced anyone disliking me before. Of course,
they might have disliked me when I won a coveted toasted teacake
for being able to spell 'knickers' in the school competition, but I had
never before experienced people disliking the idea of me.

'Eee-urgh, you're a Brit,' other kids would say when I opened
my mouth. Well, of course I was, but I wasn't sure what was wrong
with that. At school in England we hadn't studied history, but we
had grown up surrounded by the idea that Britain was a 'wonderful
thing', and that everyone was really delighted when we turned up
to colonise them. After all, they got the Queen, the English language, the right sort of people in charge and civilisation.

In my Irish history book, which had been handed down from
previous students (in the days before educational companies realised
there was profit in obsolescence) there were underlined passages to
learn by heart: about how the English kept the Irish 'poor, igno-
rant and obedient' to their Protestant masters. A dutiful student, and
keen to please, I learned these phrases with the best of them, but I
was uncomfortable. Was I really personally responsible for all these
terrible things? It felt that way.

The unrelenting awfulness of what my people had done, as told through the history book, was leavened slightly by another owner having taken his or her felt-tip pens to a sketch of Daniel O'Connell. After that, I never was able to think of the Liberator without his lipstick, beads and feather boa, as Danny La Rue.

Learning Irish was a surprise. Most of the other kids were bored of standing up for *Comhrá* by the time I came to school, but I was agog. Stories of Oisín and Niamh and Tír na nÓg were enthralling, and Irish was the only way to discover them. I picked it up quickly. Apparently, I spoke Irish 'like the Queen', which wasn't necessarily a compliment. It would be at least three decades before Elizabeth came here and wooed us all with her *cúpla focail*.

No, the only words I had in a truly Irish accent were the ones I learned here in Ireland, words that I would never have used with such colourful abandon back in England. They mainly had four letters, and could be liberally peppered, I discovered, mid-sentence, even mid-word.

I discussed things with my brother. Two years older, and charismatic by nature, he didn't seem quite so afflicted by the people disliking his part in the eight hundred years of oppression thing. I was also perturbed by the idea of the land of saints and scholars. We were already discovering the disconcertingly alien-to-us culture of sin, guilt and shame. And while I was coming quickly to realise that imperialism and colonialism weren't shiny things of joy; what was happening in the North seemed pretty wretched too. On all sides.

'You know what, Gem, maybe we need to make up our own minds,' my brother sagely said. A valuable thing to learn at the age of nine.

Ireland in 1977 didn't have the English high street stores, so people seemed to make things up for themselves, which turned out to be much more fun. I did miss dark chocolate digestive biscuits and ready-salted crisps. The money was gorgeous. Not being stuck with the Queen, the Irish pound notes were practically poetic. Charles Haughey became Minister for Health and we all got green toothbrushes, which were really crappy and the bristles fell out. We went to the Spring Show at the RDS and marvelled at the horses and farm machinery, so close to the city centre.

I couldn't live in the UK any more. Did Thatcher change England, or did Ireland change me? It had taken a little while, but oh I loved Ireland: the omnipresence of poetry and song as part of a way of life. I loved my new friends (who had by then stopped calling me a Brit, and started calling me Gemma). I loved the stories, the landscape, the way of thinking that sometimes comes at you sideways, surprising with new ideas. I loved the maverick way with words, over and above the practice of punctuating everything with expletives. I discovered that 'giving out' meant 'telling off', that never saying a definite 'no' or 'yes' was infinitely beguiling and gave huge space for improvisation.

I loved the beginning of a long, and lifetime process of realising that there are always more than two sides to everything, that national culture is itself a knotty, sometimes treacherous concept, in all its guises. And yes, I did get a pony. And I did love him too, very much indeed. And I have continued, ever since, to love finding more and more in this unexpectedly extraordinary place – that I call home.

II
1978-1987

Setting the Scene

Mary O'Malley

I don't remember the late 1970s in Ireland, not for the usual reasons, but because I wasn't there. I had left by then, and would stay away until 1986.

This period falls for me, and for a great many others, into two Irelands, and two realities. A bit like Flann O Brien's crack that de Valera had set up the Institute for Advanced Studies to prove the existence of God and St Patrick and that they had discovered there was no God and two St Patricks. There was the Ireland we left and the one we came back to. I went to Lisbon, via London. There was a play running in London called *Once a Catholic*. The title was from the old saying: 'Once a Catholic, always a Catholic.'

Being Irish was like that. You left, but you never got away. No matter how long you lived in Boston, which was normal if you came from Connemara; Berlin, which was approved in certain circles; or Lisbon – going to Lisbon was just plain awkward – as if you went specifically to court attention, like deciding to be a nun. No matter how long you were away, nobody ever asked you much about it when you came back, as if you'd been in gaol. You had become part of phantom Ireland, the one that got away and now you were back after a year, two years, ten years. So what did you think of the Pope's visit? And the new number plates on the cars. Gone was IP711 and now we had G-something or other.

That was in 1979 when I learned in a letter that 'every atheist in Ireland is up for the Pope' and heard from a man in Galway who had been forced to give up his bed to relations from the country when the Pope came to Ballybrit, and that you could smell the sausages frying from Salthill to Renmore, which, as he was a recent convert to vegetarianism, went against his religion. The car registration plates had passed me by.

In my other life we had two children, worked in a university, learned Portuguese. Learned that a woman from Inis Mór had been a nun for forty years in the Convent of Jerónimos. 'And she never lost her accent.' Did you hear about the teapot Haughey gave to Maggie Thatcher? Now what do you think of that?

And in 1981, the hunger strikes.

Ah, the hunger strikes. I heard of Bobby Sands' death on Portuguese radio and read about it in the *Diário de Notícias*. Something terrible was happening in my country and none of my friends wanted to talk about it when I went home. Then there was another kind of silence, called censorship. Ireland seemed to be slipping through a crack in time.

And Mrs Thatcher met Mr Haughey and gave him what for. Mr Haughey didn't seem very keen on her either. No more china teapots.

Sometime in the early 1980s the children of the middle classes began to leave Ireland and suddenly, emigrants were all the rage. Thousands were leaving as we came back. There was no welcome mat for the returning emigrant in Knock airport, which was officially opened in 1986. The West was a wasteland. Many who left were illegal in America, getting in through Canada, on holiday visas, doing the best they could. The human cost was stark – missed weddings and missed funerals, missed christenings and celebrations. Couples were separated, houses repossessed, marriages fell apart.

Galway University's response to the crisis on its doorstep was unique; they offered President Ronald Reagan an honorary doctorate. Pat Sheerin gave out honorary degrees on the street in protest. Christy Moore sang, *Hey Ronnie Reagan / I'm black and I'm pagan / I'm gay and I'm left and I'm free.*

Back in the real world, people mostly pulled together. Groups formed for peace, to lobby for divorce, to lobby for emigrant visas. The government helped – nobody really wanted the emigrants back, and nobody wanted to give them the vote. Other groups formed, appalled at what was being done in Latin America under US government anti-communist policy. In Galway, Adam and Eve appeared briefly in the altogether, the League of Decency objected, as did a councillor concerned for the morals of Galway. Galway Writers' workshop flourished and Jessie Lendennie set up Salmon Press in the middle of a recession. The unemployed had a voice and a centre.

In 1987 Enniskillen was bombed. Eleven more dead and sixty-three injured. Something shifted. It was the beginning of the end of the war.

There was a new Christmas song released the following year. I first heard it one cold day in December . . . *the boys of the NYPD choir were singing 'Galway Bay' . . . and the bells were ringing out for Christmas Day.*

Summer of Love and Toast

Donal Hayes

The flirting came as a surprise as we linked up for 'The Siege of Ennis'.

Dancing, weaving, moving in time since time began, eyes and smiles and hearts locked, sunlit shafts in the warm August, Irish college evening.

Later, we kissed, my first kiss ever, at fourteen.

My summer of love in Ballingeary in 1978 had started off quite bleakly. The rain was incessant, constantly whispering all day and the nights sounding only of water. I was billeted with a different *bean an tí* than my friends and it did not suit. Seventeen of us queued up at the door of Bean Uí Shuilleabháin on *an chéad lá* and, as I looked at the modest house, I couldn't believe there to be sufficient bedrooms for us all. There weren't.

The Ó Súilleabháin family (four *páistí* plus mister and missus) gamely packed into one bedroom and the seventeen *buachaillí* were bunked down in bedrooms and corridors and living rooms. As the month of August progressed the damp house ripened in sympathy to the hedgerows and a deep earthy, mushroomy, wet-leaved smell pervaded all.

Catering was a spectacular affair. Not so much for the quality, which was shocking, but for the sheer volume of food Bean Uí Shúilleabháin could produce from her limited stretch of Formica. She could produce thirty slices of warm toast at the same time from a two-slice toaster. An apparently small pot steamed scores of freshly dug *prátaí* to stomach-popping perfection. Pounds of blistering sausages all from the one pan.

There was little to entertain in Ballingeary. Every day there was a cycle to Gougane Barra and every evening a football match or a *céilí* in the hall. Curtains would be closed but spotlights of evening sunlight picked out the dancing dust.

Emer had spoken to me for the first time late in the month. The cycle to Gougane took the most beautiful twisting route to the south of the Lee although the river was still in its infancy here so it was hard to think of it as the river I walked past every day in Cork. I was at the back of the group when I realised someone was cycling beside me.

'Hey, careful, don't crash into me.'

'I'm sorry, I didn't see you,' I apologised, even though I was nowhere near her.

'Are you from here?' Her accent was clearly Dublin. One of the girls staying up at Bean Uí Mhurchú's.

'God no, you must be kidding, I'm from Cork.'

'This is Cork, ya culchie.'

'No way, Cork is the city, this is just the county. This is like, Kerry.'

Emer was poking fun at me and continued to do so for the rest of the day. I was having the most fun I had all summer and it was with a girl. My head was in a whirl. She was slightly taller than me but managed to look petite. She had the most beautiful eyes and she was laughing at everything I said. I was not stupid, I knew straight away that we were in love. I would need to tell my parents and move to Dublin.

That night was the last *céilí*, or *céilí mór*. All the *múinteoirí*, all the families and all the students would be there for one final knees-up. The whole building shook as the eight musicians on the stage launched into 'Balla Luimnigh'. Couples facing couples advancing and retiring, crossing over, crossing back, all the time holding hands. I saw Emer down the hall and tried to manoeuvre towards here but the military precision of the dance forbade it. Between the dances I was gone. Making my way down the hall through 'The Rakes of Mallow', 'The Bridge of Athlone' and 'The Humours of Bandon'. I thought I had lost her but she appeared by my side right in time for 'The Siege of Ennis'.

No one else existed. We laughed and danced, drew close and pulled away, there was sidestepping and ducking through arches and we held hands like we would never let go. As the 'Siege' ended our momentum kept us going and we ended up alone outside in the warm evening air. When we kissed my life changed. It was the single most beautiful, most delicate, most personal thing that had ever happened to me.

What ever happened to my first love?

Freagra: She is married in Perth, is still beautiful and every St Patrick's Day in the club when they play 'The Siege of Ennis' she has to step outside. She closes her eyes and runs her fingers through your soft curls and kisses your milky breath one more, gentle time.

12A

Mia Gallagher

Memory is a mushy thing. It smushes the past together, pulls it part. I used to take pride in my razor-sharp recall, but now, at fifty-one, I'm just like everyone else. The stuff that's less important has grown fuzzy at the edges; leaving isolated bright patches, like a dream that I have to focus, very hard on, to see.

Apart from the Pope's visit, I can't remember much of what happened in the world in 1979. Probably because I was too young to be aware of it. But, also because in my own private universe, so much was going on. My best friend Rosemary had left for secondary school a year early, stranding me. We had a new teacher – well-meaning but inexperienced. Under his less-than-iron rule, the tougher kids in class were quick to wreak havoc. Picking on the isolated, uncool ones like me. Physically I was changing too. At eleven I had spurted up to an almost impossible five foot nine. I tried to hide my height behind a pair of silver-framed glasses but this only made me more of a target. Nana Mouskouri, they started calling me, and not just the tougher kids. Then, into this maelstrom of uncertainty, strode Danny and Sandy and their hotbed of summer lovin'.

Grease was released in September 1978 in Ireland, but it played here for months. In our school, *Grease* fever reached its peak in early 1979. Everyone was going to the movie, queuing up at the Adelphi on Abbey Street to get in, or had seen it. Everyone knew the storyline, the names of the characters, the song lyrics. Everyone – and you can guess what's coming – except me. I came from an unconventional household. We never watched *Top of the*

Pops because we only had RTÉ. Our preferred radio station was BBC4 and our record collection was full of classical and jazz and some trad from my parents' party days hanging out with The Dubliners. The only halfway cool things there were a Leonard Cohen album and the soundtrack to *The Jungle Book*.

For months I begged my parents to let me see *Grease*. It was a 12A cert, so I needed them, or another adult, to accompany me. I was so uncool I didn't even think of trying to bunk into the cinema on my own. I cried, I pleaded. I said everyone was going, why not me. My mother spoke in the same kind voice she'd used the first time she'd tried to explain sex. Darling, she said, we need to have a chat about peer pressure. You're an individual. You shouldn't feel you have to do something just because everyone else is. Then she said something about drugs. I didn't care about individuality or peer pressure. I was ready to suck up anything that would help me belong.

But my parents didn't relent. And by April, when I'd turned twelve and could have gone on my own, *Grease* had stopped playing in the cinemas. I resigned myself. I would have to make do with reading fellow outcast Jackie Pomeroy's photo-novel of the movie.

Then, just when it all seemed over, a group of my classmates came to me. They'd decided to perform 'Summer Lovin'' for our class before the end of the school year, when we'd all separate to go to secondary school. Our inexperienced teacher had said yes. I'm not sure why they approached me. I loved acting but I wasn't a great singer. One of the girls used to be my friend. Maybe she felt sorry for me. Or maybe – with my glasses and long brown hair – I was the only obvious choice for Frenchy, the most uncool of the Pink Ladies.

We practised in the playground, every breaktime we could. I sang my heart out with Sandy and the other Pink Ladies, while the boys gave the T-Birds all the *'well a well a well a'* they could muster. Shortly after our performance, school broke up. Most of those kids I've never seen again. There's only one name I remember, but I'm not sure now she was in that group. Like I say, memory is mushy.

That autumn I started secondary school. I had a miserable first year. I was bullied for being a swot, lanky, posh, specky and hick. A real-life Sandy. The following summer I converted my flared jeans to drainpipes, ditched the glasses and, on a Kent campsite, locked eyes with my own Danny Zuko, a Boy Scout from Liverpool – or maybe it was Wales? – called Paul Modina. And though we never even kissed, I realised, for the first time, what fancying really meant. When I returned to school for the new term I told my best friend, Sharon. Tell me more, tell me more, she said.

My mum was right in lots of ways. Part of what made *Grease* a draw was the ad men telling us we had to see it and us buying into that bright dream. Our late 1970s *Aisling Gheal*. But 'Summer Lovin"' spoke to us not just because of its carefully designed retro chic or canny understanding of burgeoning sexuality. It articulated, with a dark, comic precision, that rite of passage all twelve-year-olds must undergo, not just the outsiders. Find a mask the tribe will accept, and wear it, because if you don't, you won't survive.

Wailing Like Banshees

Pat Boran

Where the monks of Skellig Michael had their beehive huts and the wailing of Atlantic winds with which to seek their moment of transcendence, back in 1980, aged seventeen and still in school, my own impulse was about as far from the hermetic as it's possible to go. Yet even so, one October night my school friend Brian and I – two young midlanders astray in an inhospitable capital city – came close to what can only be described as our own transcendent experience. Fittingly, it came about thanks to the urban equivalent of the beehive hut – and a variety of wailing that would put the Atlantic itself to shame.

By way of background, 1980 was only a couple of years after the punk revolution first upset the UK music charts and scandalised the nation with its zips and safety pins, its provocative lyrics and anti-establishment attitude. If its moment had more or less passed by now, for those bands prepared to travel to Dublin or Belfast or Cork, the enthusiasm of Irish audiences recalled the heady, inspiring days of the birth of the movement itself.

For those with an interest in such trivia, nowadays 17 October 1980 has an almost legendary glow about it: the day those darlings of the British music press, Siouxsie and the Banshees, played live in a Dublin suburban cinema. At the time it was simply the first outing for my schoolmate Brian and myself, along with a third friend, Paschal, who – as it happened – wouldn't quite make it to our particular moment of enlightenment. More of which anon.

As it happened, things started well. We located the unlikely venue of the Grand Cinema in Cabra easily enough, by following the increasingly dense population of black-clad, stud-encrusted figures drifting through the northside city streets. And of the event itself I'm sure I recall dry ice. And strobe lightning. Chants of 'Siouxsie, Siouxsie, Siouxsie!' from the impatient crowd. Tension in the air. When the band at last came on, the audience went berserk. Someone climbed on stage. Kohl-eyed, B-movie extra Siouxsie seemed upset. At the foot of the stage a couple of pogo dancers, leaping like Maasai warriors, were joined by the larger group of punks usually found outside Freebird Records on Grafton Street, their towering, glue-sculpted mohawks flashing above their heads like blades. 'Suburban Relapse'. 'Nicotine Stain'. 'Premature Burial' . . . Despite the grim titles and the downbeat rhythms, the atmosphere that filled the space usually reserved for family enter-tainment was electric, perversely uplifting.

But Siouxsie herself seemed – if one can say it of a goth – some-what off-colour, out of sorts. The drums pounded, the guitars, as promised, swirled and grated, but before we knew it they were done, and we were pouring out again onto Quarry Road – no encore, a somewhat hostile mood rippling through the disappointed crowd. And somehow Brian and I lost sight of Paschal. And it was in Paschal's aunt's flat in town that we'd been planning to spend the night . . .

For a minute we wondered if the prospect of a punk invasion was more than the poor woman could face. (And who would have blamed her?) But with no address or phone number, what choice did we have but to cut our losses. And so, shortly after our first big gig in the big smoke, we made our way back to the Liffey and out along the quays towards Heuston Station, hoping to hitch a lift to Portlaoise, therein to regale all those we'd meet with the tale of our wondrous exploits.

It was well after midnight, and somewhere between Kilmainham and the Long Mile Road, that we realised the game was up. For one thing it was dark, and we were dressed in black. It was then we spotted, glinting with frost to the side of the road, a small council or telecom workers' hut, a basic wooden frame with a corrugated roof and door which, as luck would have it, had been left unlocked.

Shovels and spools of cable. Hard hats and pliers. Already chilled to the bone and fighting back the hunger, we settled in to spend the night, lying on the bare wooden benches of our own small beehive hut that might have been on an island at the edge of the world.

And to keep from freezing, all night long we stamped and clapped our hands, singing at the tops of our voices every song we loved (by all the young punks and outcasts like ourselves – 'Pretty Vacant', 'Hit Me with Your Rhythm Stick', 'C'Mon Everybody)'; and then, when they ran out, all the hits from daytime radio we'd never have admitted to liking, let alone to knowing all the words of 'Good Times', 'Born to Be Alive', 'Let's All Chant' by The Michael Zager Band, and, okay, Queen's 'We Will Rock You'.

Back Home in Derry

John Connell

When I was a younger man I lived for a time with the Aboriginal people of Northern Australia. In the remote communities of Daguragu and Kalkarindji I met fellow travellers through history and souls of the *sean-nós*.

I was but twenty-one and Jack Bulla eighty-two but together we talked and found in one another a connection beyond the purposes that had brought me there. He was the sole survivor of a British massacre that had killed Gurdinji and Warlpiri people at Wave Hill station in the 1920s. He had learned the language of his people, its customs and most importantly their songs. He was the holder of so much memory.

The world began in song, he told me as we talked together that night. Songs are what make us who we are, he said, looking up to the outback stars. We must sing our world continually into existence.

Song, it seems to me now, is the *draíocht* of both our peoples.

We talked long into the night of freedom and then with the pull of lands so strong we too began to sing. Our words were clear and true for they were songs not of performance but ones of belonging.

When Jack finished he turned to me asking me of the songs of my land.

When I was a boy I learned of Ireland, but I did not know the story of the North. It was not taught in school, there were no great texts of that place, only a great silence. But song has always been a way to remember. On our island it was song that brought this year to me and song that forever enshrines it in the mind.

I began to unfurl the words of Bobby Sands' 'Back Home in Derry'.

They were words of the exiled Irish who had come to this great southern land in chains. Jack listened to me then as I tripped on the words, for I thought of all the suffering our peoples had endured and I thought too of 1981 and Bobby's death.

A boy can become a man in sixty-six days. A man can become a martyr. And a martyr can become a symbol for all that is wrong on one small island.

The choices that were not taken by the British are remembered now. The wrong choice or rather the unwillingness to make the right one lead boys to become offerings. Tragic choices begat real certainties. Life became death and death became politics.

'Back Home in Derry' were the modern words of the ancient, unstoppable movement of a people towards a concept; freedom.

In Sanskrit the word 'martyr' translates as that which is remembered and something that is written down and continually revised. Each generation bringing new readings and new ears to the stories of old. Raking through the lyrics of the past to find new meaning for an uncertain world.

The death of Sands like the other hunger strikers provoked silence in the British government, silence that was deafening, but his songs echoed beyond the veil, speaking of things greater than himself, leading all the way to a desert night in the Australian outback to an old Aboriginal man and me.

We sang our worlds though disparate in kind into existence again that night. From scrub bush to emerald green. From *terra nullius* to Éireann grá. To Jack his songlines sifted over the grounds not just of creation but those of bloodshed and loss, so too it was with my song.

Seamus Heaney talked of the peoples of this island living in a place of resolved contradiction but it was not just the north and south. Jack lived it too. Aboriginal and Australian, celebrated but maligned, wanted but despised. His march towards freedom took the form of a land rights movement. Sands in starvation. Sands died for a yet imagined land. Jack's struggle for a real one. That one exists and the other does not belongs to history now. Which was right and which was wrong? All that's left now is song.

The marks of the chains and the cries of the wains are still upon Jack's people as they are alike with us like shadows on our souls.

The road of life is the same road everywhere and it can point to the salvation of ourselves from our histories.

It was that road that brought Jack and I together and that same road that brought the empire and these new songs into our lives.

I sang of a home I missed. He sang of a land unfree. It was 2008. I sang of a home I missed. He sang of a land unfree. It was 2008 but that night it was 1981.

Days of 1982

Michael O'Loughlin

On the first day of January, 1982, I woke up half frozen, on the sofa in a friend's cottage in North Strand, and considered my situation: I had no money, no job and nowhere to live. I had just returned from a couple of years spent in Copenhagen and Barcelona, oscillating between the two in a rehearsal of my future life, in which I would always seem to be swinging back and forth between north and south, blue and red, heart and head, the Baltic and the Med. But I was not downcast. I had published a slim volume of poetry the year before, and was working on another one, equally slim, about which I was very excited. However, there was still the small problem of a place to live.

I had been in vague contact with Bernard Loughlin, due to our shared passion for Barcelona. I had heard about this new place, a retreat for artists somewhere down the country, and Bernard, somewhat improbably, was its first director. So I called him. 'Sure. Come on up,' was his immediate reaction, in those staccato Belfast tones, which would become familiar to a generation of Irish writers and artists. And I did. His wife Mary picked me up in Dublin and we drove north to the Tyrone Guthrie Centre at Annaghmakerrig, to the house that would be my home for the next three months.

There were only a couple of other people there, as the artistic community was still a little wary. It seemed almost too good to be true: a large beautiful house in idyllic surroundings of wood and lake, with central heating (still a rarity) and all the cordon bleu food you could eat. And, if you couldn't afford the modest contribution, it was free! And nobody, apparently, could afford it. Nothing like it had been seen in Ireland before. One elderly poet there, a survivor of the tough post-war years and the dark 1950s, could occasionally be seen scurrying furtively back and forth to the kitchen, hoarding biscuits and cheese and other delicacies in his room, as if terrified that someone might suddenly wake up and padlock the kitchen.

Taking the first step as an artist is the result of a visceral need – but to continue meaningfully, you will need support and nurture, and Annaghmakerrig under Bernard always gave you the sense that what you were engaged in was not just important, it was the most vital activity in the world. Bernard was all about the artist, and believed that nothing was too good for the creating classes.

He presided genially, if not always gently, over the dinner table in the evening, where everything was up for debate, and no one had the right not to be offended. The one taboo was cant. On one memorable occasion, a senior arts official, a pleasant and dil-igent chap, arrived up on the Friday night, presumably to see if the taxpayer was getting value for money. He stood, back to the fire in Bernard's kitchen, as Mary cooked Spanish-style lentils, and gesturing out the window, he said in a jocular tone: 'Ah Bernard, I see you're driving a Toyota.' I will never forget the merciless tirade which followed from Bernard, beginning with the words: 'Seán: We. Are. Not. Here. To. Talk. About. Cars.'

In this stimulating environment I finished my book and wrote most of my next one. But I couldn't live in Annaghmakerrig forever, though some of my fellow artists seemed determined to do so.

I went back to a Dublin that was grey and full of derelict buildings. In 1982 Charlie Haughey was Taoiseach, and his grinning death's-head face seemed to leer out of every TV screen and newspaper. Not that the other side were any better – most politicians were keeping their heads down in the savage culture war that was going on, as dark forces sought to add a blatantly sectarian amendment to the constitution, which they succeeded in doing after a bitter referendum. We would have to wait thirty-four years to repeal it. Ireland seemed to be following its old pattern of two steps forward,

one step back. I had faith in the future, but I didn't fancy hanging around for the two steps forward. As the economy went into its regular nosedive, emigration had returned and most of my friends were gone abroad. The streets seemed empty. I had finished my new book, and I realised it was time to go back to Europe, where I would spend the next couple of decades.

In the end Bernard left Annaghmakerrig for personal reasons, and returned to his beloved Catalunya. I suspect it was a timely exit all the same, as he would have had a hard time in the era of expert advisory panels, strategy documents and a Public Accounts Committee. These days a young penniless, jobless and homeless poet might well find the Tyrone Guthrie Centre beyond his or her reach – even if there was room.

I still occasionally meet friends from those days, grizzled veterans all, at book launches, gallery openings, Aosdána assemblies, and increasingly, funerals. We were not there in the GPO in 1916, nor did we fight in the Spanish Civil War. At worst, we drank some bad red wine and shivered in unheated studios. But still, surviving the 1980s as an artist was not always easy. One thing is sure: Bernard Loughlin made it a lot easier for a lot of people.

Bomb-scare Ballerina

Martina Devlin

The season: Advent. The atmosphere: elated. The occasion: a Christmas shopping trip – my mother, sister and me go to Derry, thirty miles away.

When we step off the bus, our excitement is diluted somewhat. Derry is tense. Watchful. Only festive on the surface. The city is full of police along with – a new development – soldiers with strange accents and walkie-talkies, which snap, crackle and pop. They are cradling rifles, holding them close to their chests. I notice how the grown-ups stare at these weapons. Glance away. Can't look away – gape at them again.

Although I don't know it, my parents have discussed whether or not to proceed with this outing. Since that summer, the Troubles have been erupting around us and Derry is in a febrile condition. Today's apparent peace is conditional.

But my mother and father want us to have a normal childhood. To enjoy the pleasures of the season. They are gambling on the expedition being incident-free. A treat and not an ordeal.

I'm in Woolworth's gazing at a treasure trove: a row of ballerina fairies, each more glamorous than the last. They have silver wings, their arms are raised, one leg extends as though to spin a pirouette. Best of all are their tutus, spangled tissue paper and net in rainbow colours, which crinkles when you touch it. I burn to own one of these miraculous creatures. The numbers on the label suggest it might be possible. My life's savings are contained in the handbag I'm carrying, blue plastic with a metal Scottie dog badge on the side. I have just enough.

I look around for my mother to consult on colours. She's vanished. A momentary twinge, before I lapse back into a joyful daze, choosing which fairy to buy.

A siren jolts me from my state of bliss.

'Bomb! Everybody out!' yells a voice. 'Now! Out now! Go!' A gush of panic overwhelms the shop. Screams. Breaking glass. Pounding feet. I'm jostled. A woman's high heel lands on my toe and I cry out, but she doesn't look back. My mother rushes up, breathless, and seizes my hand. With her is my sister, her cheeks slick with tears.

We're funnelled outside. On the street, other shops are emptying, other alarms blaring. People are running, crying, shouting. We trot to the station and catch the next bus home to Omagh. I spend the entire journey worrying about the ballerinas. Will they be blown up? Will their pointy legs be separated from their elegant bodies, their tutus and wings ripped apart?

On the news that evening, we discover it was a hoax bomb, so I know they're safe. Now I transfer my fretting to thwarted ownership of a fairy. Every day, I pester my mother but she's not for going back. Finally, at the start of the school holidays, she relents.

And the day arrives when I hand over my money for a fairy in a sea-green dress. On the way home, I take her out of the bag and twirl and jump her on my lap, making her dance for joy. Her leg pops off. My mother rolls her eyes. That night, my father glues it back.

Fast forward to December 1983. I am Christmas shopping in London. It's in my mind to buy a new decoration for the tree because our fairy surely must be ready for retirement. I'll pick up one in Harrods, I think, and try to buy a tube ticket for Knightsbridge. But in the underground I hear about an IRA car bomb right outside the department store. This time, there's an explosion. Destruction, devastation, death.

My mind floods with memories of that first bomb I knew of, back in Derry. Knowing my parents will have heard the news, I make a phone call to reassure them. Then I change my plans and book a plane ticket for Christmas at home.

We never do replace the ballerina. Every year since 1969, she has perched on our tree. I have her still, battered by time, like all of us: tutu faded, silver wings dog-eared, that wayward leg held into its socket with an elastic band. It wouldn't be Christmas without her. To me, she remains the epitome of beauty. In dark times and in joyful, during Troubles and peace, she has presided over our family celebrations, a symbol of goodwill and good cheer. She is hope personified, hope enduring, hope rewarded.

Each December, before I climb a ladder and set her in place, we take a twirl around the living room together ... my bomb-scare ballerina and me.

Winter Solstice

Cyril Kelly

I am standing in my mother's millinery shop. The blind is down. As if the winter solstice had entered, lingering light has settled on shelves, on the Singer sewing machine, on its cold, cast-iron treadle. Balanced on slender stems around, a flock of hats; I imagine exotic birds poised for flight. My mother's latest creations, well . . . my mother's final creations. Spread out on the counter, splashes of crimson velvet; three Christmas dresses she had made, never expecting them to be posthumous presents for our children, her granddaughters. It is December 1984 and my wife Breeda and myself have just arrived from Dublin.

Three miles outside Listowel, we stopped at the funeral home. Hardly out of the car when old Dinsey, cap at a jaunty angle shading a canny eye, stepped forward to herd me into the kitchen. In response to my grim recitative, 'Where is she?' he kept up a steady, 'No hurry no hurry at all me ould pal.' All the while busying himself, poking in cupboards, talking over his shoulder, 'Will you sit down there for a minute will you.' Until, eventually, placing a saucer of Marietta and a mug of MiWadi gallantly before Breeda, he turned to me with, 'A lovely *cailín*, your mother, a lovely *cailín* entirely,' as he pressed a brimming tumbler into my hand. My first sip had me spluttering but, regardless, Dinsey continued: 'Sure look at here, what can we say? What can we say but that she was some woman. All the ladies of seven parishes mad to be seen in one of her fancy hats.' And sampling a mouthful from his own drink, he clinked his glass to mine: 'That's the best of stuff. A drop of wine to colour the aul *poitín* for fear the law might call. It'll do you good!'

My glance hovers around the shop, alighting on ostrich feathers, ribbons, thimbles, accoutrements of the milliner's craft. It is as if she had just left everything, intending to return. Surrounded by pensive light, I recall other days, days of my childhood when that blind would also be down, the shop door shut. Ironically, as a seven-year-old, I was obsessed with funeral processions murmuring and shuffling past that very door. That succession of small white coffins of the 1950s, peals of mourning, pulsing in pairs from the belfry in The Square. Adults bewailing a litany of infant diseases: diphtheria, whooping cough, pneumonia. And my mother wrapping me in her arms to banish the Angel of Death lurking in the shadows.

And later, in my teenage years, helping my father in the sawmill behind the house, the two of us gravitating towards this place at the end of each day, a pair of Neanderthals, hoary with sawdust. After the demented siren of the circular saw, such a resonance of silence that you could hear the whispering fire. And she, seated at the counter, absorbed by that critical juncture when craft aspires to art, refusing to be distracted by my father's *Beware the needle of the stitching milliner / You risk your life if you try kissing her.* Prodding the needle through the roots of her hair for lubrication, she'd thimble it, a silvery eel, slipping and wriggling through layers of silk or lace, drawing thread after thread in a sighing arc, obsessed by that elusive notion of flair defined by grace.

Finally, when the small talk and reminiscences began to staccato towards silence, Dinsey, who had been eying my tumbler, decided that the time had come to drain his own. 'Right so,' he said, his voice softer, free of earlier bravura. 'We'll go in to see herself.'

There is no rehearsing for such a moment. You cannot re-enact those first minutes of witnessing your mother in repose. That initial addled response; a jumble of bewilderment and compassion and grief. Pulling up a couple of chairs for Breeda and myself, Dinsey left, closing the door quietly after him.

And today, looking back through the vista of years, I can see myself clearly, that evening in my mother's shop, sitting eventually on her cane chair, needing to be on my own. As the turbulence of the previous hours was beginning to subside, I was grieving not just for a mother, but also, as I looked around at shelves laden with the acumen and faded artefacts of the ages, I was lamenting the end of an era that had begun with my grandmother opening her Millinery Hall almost a century before.

So now I interrogate myself; what of that artistic heritage have I brought with me? Well, with my wife's imprimatur, I can sew a button on a shirt or pucker a patch onto the lining of a pocket if keys or coins fall through. But yet, there are mirroring moments when, after poring over a recently written paragraph, endeavouring to blend and balance each sentence for colour and rhythm and style, I sometimes glimpse a memory; my mother's relentless exactitude, rotating her latest creation at arm's length, mercilessly scrutinising every curve and fold and frill.

Moving Statues

Paul Rouse

As evening falls on 22 July 1985 three local people are walking through the dusk past a Marian shrine in the small West Cork village of Ballinspittle. They stop to say a decade of the rosary. The shrine is a beautiful one, set back into the hillside and surrounded by bushes. As the women pray, they see the statue of the Virgin Mary come alive. One of the women sees what appears to be breathing; the other two see Mary's hands appear to move. They rush to nearby houses and later that evening thirteen people all say that they have seen the statue of the Virgin Mary move. News of the moving statue in Ballinspittle is reported by the local and then the national and then the international press. First hundreds and then thousands of people begin congregating every evening. Within a month, a quarter of a million people have made their way to Ballinspittle. Hymns are sung and prayers recited; many claim to have seen the statue move. The apparition is explained as the mingling of two worlds: the real world and the mystical world. Minor miracles are reported. One woman claims to have been cured of deafness; a stroke victim is said to have been cured of paralysis. Crowds begin to congregate at Marian shrines all across Ireland. As the weeks pass, other statues in other parishes begin to move. Indeed, a certain mass hysteria sweeps villages and towns and even cities.

The classroom of 5A in Tullamore Christian Brothers School is full of boys waiting for anything to happen. There's a geography class being taught by Seamus O'Dea, the school vice principal who has taught many of our fathers. Behind him is a blackboard and

above the blackboard is a two-foot statue of the Virgin Mary, in flowing blue-and-white robes and a strange red-lipped smile.

'She's moving, sir. She definitely moved.'

'Sit down Cooney, and stop acting the galoot.'

'But, sir, I saw it too. She's swaying.'

'Should you ring RTÉ, sir?'

All across the classroom lads are staring up at the statue, trying to look angelic and awe-struck. Seamus O'Dea is doing his best not to laugh. He knows he can't turn around to look up at the statue – that would be to hand a victory to a room he must not lose to. And, anyway, he likes our class so he won't get thick with us. He knows that this, too, will pass.

Although not until it has been well milked.

'She just waved at me, sir.'

'Sir, she's breakdancing now.'

And on it goes like that for class after class, trying to get a rise out of the teachers. Someone makes a homemade *Out of Order* sign and hangs it around Mary's shoulders. It disappears when we go home for the evening.

A new sign is made. It reads: *Insert coin.* That, too, disappears in the evening.

And then the miracle happens. The Virgin Mary is carefully positioned on the edge of the blackboard. It must surely fall the first time any teacher takes a duster to the board. And fall it does – a sort of premonition of Morrissey singing 'alabaster crashes down'. It hits the floor with a thump. But the Virgin Mary stays in one piece, apparently unharmed.

'A miracle, sir. A miracle!'

'She jumped, sir. With no parachute!'

Back down in Ballinspittle, a local garda sergeant tells the press he has seen the statue move: 'Rosaries were being said, hymns were being sung. Suddenly, without warning, it was as if the statue simply took off and became airborne. I saw the concrete statue of Our Lady floating in mid-air. Not rocking to and fro, but floating.'

It is a reminder that if you look at something long enough, you can choose to see it whatever way you wish.

Now, looking back into the 1980s, looking through the school gates, past the *wedgie* tree and the smoking shed and boys playing handball in the morning and basketball after school, I see a room full of boys. There are big white boot runners and mullets and flecky trousers. All the days have been squeezed into one endless class. There's learning and laughter and messing and gear bags with dirty football boots. Nobody has a clue what is happening . . .

The Virgin Mary is standing on top of the blackboard. And we are all just waiting.

Thunderbolt

Alannah Hopkin

1986. Where to start? At the beginning, naturally, with the thunderbolt – the *coup de foudre*.

I was thirty-six, living in Kinsale, earning my living as a writer.
I had moved to Ireland from London two years before, soon after
the publication of my first novel. After some rocky times finan-
cially, I had signed a generous contract for a non-fiction book, and
had no money worries. I enjoyed Kinsale, my mother's home town,
and did not miss London at all. I had a wide circle of friends, and
a couple of boyfriends, both Dubliners, who visited occasionally.
After an intense affair with a married man, who broke my heart, and
a brief engagement to a man who had an increasingly serious drink
problem, I was glad not to be in love, to be footloose and fancy-free,
captain of my own ship.

For some weeks my friend Derek had been awaiting the arrival
of Higgins, his friend the novelist Aidan Higgins. After many years
out of Ireland Higgins was living in Wicklow. Seamus Heaney had
told him that if he returned to Ireland, he could become a founder
member of an association of writers and artists called Aosdána, and
the government would give him an annual income, provided he
dedicated himself full time to writing. He was on the next plane,
and after a quick visit to Dublin to seal the formalities, he headed
for Wicklow where his brother was living.

But after two years, Higgins was not happy in the depths of the
country. Derek immediately solved the problem: he should move
to Kinsale, which had twenty-three pubs and plenty of congenial
company. He gave Higgins my number, as someone who could

help him find a cottage with a sea view at a reasonable rent – a tall order, even in 1986. He rang me one evening; his voice was a pleasant surprise, what you would call an educated voice, more English than Irish and very serious, definitely the voice of a reader of the *Times Literary Supplement*, a man who would know a hawk from a handsaw.

Derek asked if I would help him to entertain Higgins. It was late October, but still dry and sunny. Kinsale looked gorgeous in its autumn colours, the grey stone buildings against a blue sea. 'He's coming down by helicopter,' was the latest news, followed next week by 'No sign of Higgins'. Another week went by. Then finally some news: Higgins was arriving on Wednesday, could I join them for dinner? I said I'd meet them in the bar after my swim in the hotel pool.

I remember having wet hair, and being too impatient to dry it, suddenly curious to see what Higgins looked like. Suppose, I thought idly, he turns out to be someone significant in my life, and his first view of me is of an otter-like wet head? I dismissed this untypical romantic thought from my thoroughly rational mind, and headed for the bar.

And there he was, in a wine-red sweater, medium height and build, long reddish-brown hair, beard, granny glasses, slightly stooped, engaged in close conversation with an enormous Viking called Sven. I remember Sven's handshake almost breaking my bones, while the touch of Aidan's hand was like velvet. Sven was a sea captain, Aidan told me in his extraordinary voice, who had once killed a man in the course of his duties.

We dined at the Shipwreck, a new place near the hotel. Derek did not drink wine, so Aidan and I agreed on a bottle of Rioja. Derek knew that we were both interested in the writer Malcolm Lowry, and introduced this topic. I listened to Aidan explaining a theory a Canadian friend had about Lowry. I liked the way he stood up for his friend's theory against my demolition of it. I liked the way he took me seriously, and didn't flirt. Aidan ordered another bottle of Rioja, at which point Derek politely left.

We first kissed in the street outside the Shipwreck, and Aidan's glasses fell apart. Mine often did the same, and I was able to retrieve the pieces and put them together. Aidan was struck dumb with admiration at this feat. I noticed that his eyes were hazel, exactly the same colour as mine. It was like looking into my own soul. The thunderbolt struck. I took his hand and we went back to my house, and did not see Derek again until the Saturday.

'A nice pair,' was his amused greeting, as we knocked contritely on his door. We had come to collect Aidan's things. He was moving in with me. That was 1986, and we were seldom apart until he died, holding my hand, twenty-nine years later.

An tAmhrán Bán

Doireann Ní Ghríofa

Sí an oíche a ghlaonn chuici í, an stoirm
a chumann í – fonn síoda, fonn sí

a bhí nach mór dearmadta againn.
Nuair a mhúsclaíonn sí amhrán ársa

na gcalóga sneachta, líonann béal
gach scamaill lena liricí, scaoileann siad

féileacán bán le damhsa tríd an oíche.
Eitlíonn siad ar shéideán gaoithe,

go dtiteann siad ar chrainn is ar dhíonta,
ar bhinn gach cró, gach monarchan is stábla.

Titeann siad síos, síos, síos trí shlinnte,
ceann ar cheann, go mall, mall.

Ní fios fós céard a bheidh i ndán dúinn
nuair a dhúiseoimíd, ach go mbeidh brat binn

sneachta romhainn, is beathaisnéis
an amhráin bháin breactha ann

i lorg coise an phréacháin
le caesúr is croisín, is scáil-nóta fáin.

Snow Song

Doireann Ní Ghríofa

Night begins it, this ancient blizzard,
a static hiss all fizz and whistling,

A forgotten snow song which sets skies
singing, pale and glistening.

Night draws down that old air, and when it falls,
it falls everywhere, a lilting refrain

from mouths of cloud, a chorus
of elsewheres. Its lyrics sing

a million white butterfly wings into flight,
fluttering through winds of night-ice,

to alight on the factory's peaks and gables,
icing every tree, every shed and stable.

They fall, they fall, they fall through the squall,
they slant and fall through ceiling and wall,

through rafters and beams, through eyelids,
and into our dreams.

All we know of tomorrow
is that it will gleam.

In the morning, we'll read this symphony
pressed into snow by the feet of a crow,

marked there by crotchet, caesura,
and ghost note.

III
1988-1997

Setting the Scene

Joseph O'Connor

Picture an arctic wasteland ruled by a wicked, vengeful wizard and his team of snickering hobbits with dark eyes and bad breath. Then, remove the fun. You're not far from Ireland, 1986. A country where excitement was constitutionally illegal, unless you happened to be a sheep or a nun.

Unemployment was high. Confidence was low. The rain fell horizontally. Zombies roamed the land. It took four and a half hours to drive from Dublin to Athlone. A banshee would be waiting when you got there.

Things like self-esteem were not felt to be useful. Teachers were not passive-aggressive, they were aggressive. It saved time. The wind moaned all night, in the voice of Charlie Haughey. A plane ticket to London cost five hundred pounds so most of us went on the ferry.

That is my main memory of mid-1980s Ireland. Loss, country music and seasickness.

The ship would roll and rock its way across the Irish Sea, as other ships had done for hundreds of years, loaded with youthful hope and Tayto.

In the middle of the night, you'd arrive into Holyhead, the ugliest town in Britain. There you'd trudge past the line of surly-looking customs officers or Special Branch detectives and board the train for one of England's cities. And somewhere before dawn, a strange miracle would happen: things would start to feel a bit better.

The train would cross Britain's midlands, past the factories and farmlands, the motorways sleeping in their sodium glare, and the million lights of London would loom in the distance. You were young, full of excitement at the things that might happen. Little things like a job. A private life.

Everyone, perhaps, has a London of their own, made of images and memories as much as places. The wonderful little bookshops of Charing Cross Road, the great peacefulness of all places where old books are gathered. Lord Nelson looking down haughtily on the pigeons of Trafalgar Square. Nightclubs, coffee bars, the walk by the Thames. Punks in Chelsea, shaggy with aplomb. Galleries. Museums. The British Library in Bloomsbury. The house where Yeats lived. The grave of Karl Marx. Virginia Woolf's Bloomsbury, her ghost in every doorway. The sinful streets of Soho, glowing neon in the rain.

The Comedy Club in a cellar on Leicester Square, where, for the princely sum of two pounds on a Sunday night, you would see bright young hopefuls like Paul Merton or Jo Brand and hope not to get picked on by one of them. 'I remember you from my last gig,' Jo Brand said to me, one night from the stage. 'In a certain light you might be mistaken for handsome.'

The music shops on Denmark Street, windows squiggling with saxophones. A night in the French House pub, when I glanced up and noticed, in a corner, Robert Plant of Led Zeppelin, looking leaner and healthier than those half his age in the bar. I have seen more fat on a chip.

I think of that decade in my life as one of goings and returnings, of never being quite sure of my homeplace. Often, in London, I felt I belonged, as so many hundreds of thousands of the Irish have done, down the years. Even London's place-names seemed poetry. To this day, I cannot hear the words 'Piccadilly' or 'Primrose Hill' without experiencing that strange ache of longing with which we remember youth. Sometimes, back in Dublin for a weekend or Christmas, I'd feel an odd kind of loneliness, because all of my friends had left. I would like to say that I noticed at the time how the country was evolving and changing, but in all truth I didn't, it felt the same as it ever was.

But in November 1990 Mary Robinson was elected president, a momentous event in itself but also a marker of tectonic movement, and the changes grew impossible not to see. And impossible things were happening. There was confidence, hopefulness. A process began that would lead to the Good Friday Agreement. And on the personal front, lights were about to switch on.

In 1994 I met the most beautiful and charismatic Londoner I had ever seen in my life. On the evening I met her, she was about to go on a date. She told me she would never go out with me, that I wasn't her type. We've now been married for twenty years.

Certain friends I remember now disappeared into London. They never came back, and some of us lost touch. I hope England was kind to them, as it was to me, in those years. I don't think any of us envisaged the strange, new country we inhabit now in Ireland, where you can't smoke in a pub but you can buy a condom and a croissant in a petrol station. It's a long way from a train in the middle of the night, crossing England's midlands like a rumour.

A Year of Magic

Dermot Bolger

Everyone should have one year as special as 1988 was to me. A year when I felt at my most vibrant and every day resonated with possibilities. A hinge year when imperceptibly I entered a new phase of life.

Dublin decreed 1988 to be that city's thousandth anniversary. To celebrate every family received a Millennium milk bottle, brimming with milk and embossed with the city's crest: an heirloom designed to be passed down to future generations. If nothing else, this allowed us to partake in the Irish tradition of drinking our way through family heirlooms.

But for me 1988 was the year I finished a novel; the year I bought a house almost by accident; the year we decided to get married but almost forgot to; the year when, as a publisher, I risked publishing Paddy Doyle's memoir, *The God Squad*: a book so controversial our usual printers wouldn't print it. The year I readied myself to become a husband and a father.

The year when I proposed to my girlfriend, suggesting that sometime later that year we'd hold a simple ceremony to mark a bond of love that needed no legal document to make it feel permanent. The year when we chanced to pass a small house for sale and bid on it, so naive that we regarded the massive pool where birds bathed on the shed roof as picturesque and not evidence that the roof might collapse.

In later years, bidding on larger houses, we entered a Kafkaesque world of three-card trickery with a new breed of estate agents. They seemed utterly different from the resolutely decent estate agent who phoned me two nights after we bid on the house to give his word that, if I matched the asking price, the house was ours, with no further chicanery entertained.

The decency underpinning this transaction meant that when the sellers were delayed in moving into their new home, we thought nothing of ignoring legal advice and letting them stay for a spell in their old home, after we purchased it. They repaid our concern with concern for us that when winter came – the former owner arrived every evening to light our anthracite-burning stove, which he claimed was difficult to light.

I hadn't the heart to tell him he was lighting it wrong. I'd wait until he left before I lit it properly. He was so generous it felt rude to start without him. Moving into an old house can feel eerie. But no house needs a poltergeist when it has an anthracite stove. Some winter nights I'd wake to find that the anthracite embers had miraculously reared up into such flames that the water tank in the attic seemed about to explode. I'd race into the garden in my underpants to scatter blazing anthracite on the grass where it glistened like the lights of stars being extinguished.

Owning a house felt new and exhilarating. But everything felt exhilarating about 1988, which flew past so quick that only in early December did my girlfriend say, 'Aren't we meant to get married this year?' Thankfully there is a poets' mafia. One poet, a gentle priest, offered to marry us at two weeks' notice at the side altar of an ancient church: no mass, just a blessing, an exchange of vows and poems by Osip Mandelstam. Another poet, the late Conleth O'Connor, drove us around hotels which sought a king's ransom to host our reception. Another poet, the late Philip Casey, suggested that the wonderful Kevin Connolly who ran the Winding Stair Bookshop might let us celebrate our wedding there. Another poet arranged a superb caterer at short notice. A mechanically competent poet rigged up kegs of Guinness.

Like everything that year, it seemed impossible to organise in time but on 17 December we walked up the aisle together: nobody giving anybody away. A consortium converged on the

Winding Stair Bookshop: poets and actors; lads I played football with; nurses who'd trained with my wife; family and friends. Every poet present vowed unfaithfully to help Kevin Connolly, who owned The Winding Stairs, to clean up.

Gay Byrne curtailed our honeymoon when he suddenly interviewed Paddy Doyle on *The Late Late Show*. Ireland was mesmerised by this heroic wheelchair-bound man describing being a child abused in Catholic orphanages and hospitals. The first chink appeared in the wall of silence surrounding institutional abuse.

Despite fears of losing our new house by being sued by the hospitals Paddy condemned, we were so swamped by orders for his book that, three days after getting married, we sat putting dust jackets on *The God Squad* and wheeling boxes on bicycles down to bookshops. Everything felt imbued with change as we lived that golden year to the full, immersed in its rich possibilities, with no sense of tragedies to come.

The Land of Lost Content

Conall Hamill

For me, 'the blue remembered hills' of childhood, 'the land of lost content', are in the townland of Lylo and the farm where my mother was born. As townlands go, it's rather small: not much more than a hundred acres of what I always thought of as peaceful farm-land located between Portadown and Lurgan. My early years were punctuated by frequent trips up there. Despite the tedium of the ninety-mile car journey from Dublin and the interminable delays at the Killeen border crossing, we lived for these visits. It was a different world: the shop near the top of the lane sold Opal Fruits and HP sauce, gastronomic delights hard to find in the 'Free State'. My aunt cooked ceaselessly: tasty stews, griddle bread and apple tarts. Then there was my uncle who, in the days long before anyone had thought of welding the words 'health' and 'safety' into a single concept, cheerfully encouraged my brother and me to cling precar-iously to his tractor as he trundled across fields to check on cattle.

There were other differences. Sometimes their language fell strangely on my Dublin ears. My aunt would warn us not to fall into the *sheugh*. She would invite us to the table with an unfamiliar form of the imperative: 'Sit you down there now.' My uncle's hearty greeting, 'What about ye?', or his suggestion that we should go for 'a wee dander' had me perplexed. Other things had me perplexed too, like the group of men we passed in nearby Clanrolla who spent hours beating drums with a frenzied passion in the heat of early July.

Occasionally, after the Troubles had started, I detected an urgency in my uncle's voice as he advised my father on the best route to take on the journey back south, his strangely lengthened vowels adding a weight of meaning that I didn't fully understand: 'Och, ye don't want to go by Taaandrageee.' I had my own reasons for being suspicious of Tandragee: that was where they made porridge oats, the raw materials of my least favourite breakfast. But this seemed insufficient grounds for avoiding it: after all, you were hardly going to be force fed porridge as you drove through. A few times, in the early 1970s, my uncle drove ahead of us on our journey home, nearly as far as Poyntzpass, his northern registration providing diplomatic immunity, as he saw it, for our vulnerable southern-registered car. Gradually, I began to realise that there was something else different about my uncle's and aunt's lives: as it was for Seamus Heaney, so too all around them … the ministry of fear.

As I grew older, and the violence intensified, I slowly became aware of how much had been concealed from us as children. My bucolic version of the North was not the complete truth. I was in my twenties before I discovered that my grandfather had once received an anonymous note telling him to stay away from an auction for land adjoining his farm. He obeyed the warning.

I was thirty years old when I learned that when my uncle finally abandoned the, by then, dilapidated farmhouse and moved to the other side of Portadown, someone hung a sign near the gateway that read *Good Riddance*.

That was 1989 – and not very long after that awful event that seemed to underline how different life was in the North. Two off-duty British Army soldiers drove into the route of an IRA funeral in Belfast, apparently by mistake. Fearing a repetition of a Loyalist attack that had taken place at another IRA funeral only three days earlier, members of the cortège surrounded the car. The images, captured by TV cameras, press photographers and army helicopters, shocked the world. The crowd smashed the windows, pulled the two men from the vehicle, beat them mercilessly and then bundled them into a black cab to be taken away and shot. The journalist Mary Holland witnessed one of the soldiers being dragged to his death. She wrote in *The Irish Times*: 'He didn't cry out, just looked at us with terrified eyes as though we were enemies in a foreign country who wouldn't have understood what language he was speaking if he called out for help.'

But two other, equally powerful, images of that event linger. Fr Alec Reid is kneeling over the body of one of the men. Thinking he was still alive, he had given him the kiss of life. The soldier's blood that stains the priest's mouth may look grotesque but implies a gesture of supreme compassion, the same compassion that moved two local women to place a coat over one of the dead bodies, saying: 'He was somebody's son.' With those two gestures, we were reminded that maybe we're not really that different after all.

Event TV

Brian Leyden

It is June 1990 and, at the Sacred Heart Church in Roscommon and St Patrick's Church Athleague, Saturday evening mass times have been brought forward to seven o'clock to avoid a clash with the World Cup quarter-final kick off at eight o'clock, when Ireland take on host nation Italy.

In Ireland's first-ever appearance at the World Cup, Jack Charlton's team have done better than anyone anticipated; with 1–1 draws against England and Holland, a scrappy deadlock with Egypt, and a penalty shootout against Romania that concludes with a thrilling Packie Bonner save and David O'Leary goal.

Above the roars of 'Olé, olé, olé' and 'Oh! Ah! Paul McGrath!' the operatic scale of the romance is heightened by the BBC's inspired decision to have Pavarotti sing *Nessun Dorma* as the signature tune for their coverage.

Early mass, and the prayers of the Roscommon faithful, do nothing unfortunately to stop Schillaci pouncing on a rebound to boot the ball into the back of the net and bury Ireland's hopes.

Ray Houghton's goal against Italy in our opening World Cup game in the USA in 1994 makes it seem like, but doesn't quite deliver on, a promised repeat of Italia '90.

There had been a more truly spontaneous moment of euphoria that same year, when the crowd sprang to its feet to applaud Riverdance at the Eurovision Song Contest won by Paul Harrington and Charlie McGettigan's performance of 'Rock & Roll Kids'. But the Eurovision was no longer quite the beacon television event it used to be, except perhaps for the voting to see who got a resounding *douze points!* Or to see the French give the UK a derisory *un point.*

Think back though to watching the Dublin Horse Show, with Paul Darragh and Eddie Macken on Boomerang, and the heart-stopping instant of a bar rattled but still 'in the cup' for a clear round competing for the Aga Khan Trophy – the very name as exotic as Coleridge's *Kubla Khan* and the RDS a pleasure dome to equal Xanadu itself.

And as we also had a high-gain aerial pointed towards Enniskillen we got to enjoy the legendary grunt and grudge matches on the centre court at Wimbledon with Borg or Agassi slugging it out, and that indelibly inked roll-call of giants of event TV – John McEnroe's 'You cannot be serious!' when the umpire adjudged the ball 'Out!' Graf, Evert, Wade, Navratilova. Hurricane Higgins losing it, and Dennis Taylor winning it in the Crucible.

On RTÉ, event TV came in the form of the annual *Rose of Tralee* contest, and heated debates impishly stoked by host Gay Byrne on *The Late Late Show.* And not since the nation puzzled over how Jim Figgerty got the figs into the fig rolls, or a soldier bereft of an egg to fry on the hot desert stones recalled Sally O'Brien 'and the way she might look at you' was there such a signal moment in event TV as when the question arose: 'Who shot JR?'

You may say we were fools to fall for such conspicuous marketing. But event TV was in essence a joyously engrossing affair: a communal engagement with the likes of Edward Haley's *Roots* and the blood feud between the Ewing and Barnes families in *Dallas*, a TV series that so preoccupied the nation a joke went around that the nightly weather forecast was obliged to keep us up to date with Sue Ellen's gin intake.

Not that the swaggering, highly-sexed denizens of Southfork Ranch, along with the steamy goings-on of a cleric in the Australian outback of the earlier *Thorn Birds* TV saga didn't present problems for parents with youngsters glued to the small screen.

So when a couple undressed, climbed into bed and got notably active under the sheets my mother was obliged to tell us children they were 'searching for their pyjamas'.

1990 of course saw the arrival of the first portable computer, the laptop – a straw in the wind that would, over the decade that began the countdown to the Millennium, swallow up what I look back on now as the glory days of event TV.

Though it occurs to me that what I am really seeing is a cath-ode-ray beam lighting up the ghosts of my past, and the true event is that every one of my family, including the dog on the hearth rug with her head tight up to the fire, is still alive and cosily gathered in our sitting room, close together and unthinkingly happy as we share a supper of spaghetti hoops on toast, awaiting next week's instal-ment as that spot in the middle of the television shrinks to nothing and the screen goes blank.

What's in a Name

Anne Marie Kennedy

In 1991, when my eight-year-old marriage died, one of the things I missed most was my name. I wanted to relinquish the one I took in signing the register but there was no easy accommodation for reverting to the maiden one.

I also lost my status. I was no longer 'Mrs' but at thirty-one years old felt I couldn't be 'Miss' either.

Beginning the next chapter of my life I went to live in a rented cottage. One of the first things I bought was a good electric blanket, the bitter-sweet symbolism realised, the elation soon dampened when I read the electrical guarantee card, which had to be handed back to the retailer: *Mr, Mrs* or *Miss* boxes glowed accusingly at me from the dressing table, waiting for a decision, a ticked declaration that could make a liar out of me. I cried in my warm, loft bed.

The Eircom man who came to install the phone blushed when asking if I was 'On my own, married or what?'

'Or what?' I said, twisting the non-existent ring on my third finger.

I had to notify the car insurance company of my address change; they suggested leaving well enough alone name-wise, as did the dentist's receptionist and the travel agent. Because I worked in the bank, I was spared the awkwardness of account-opening bureaucracy.

Needless to say, there were a few tragicomic name-related encounters. I took boots for repair to a cobbler, a simple man called Tommy, a man who knew me well. 'What'll it be?' he said, as if I was ordering a cocktail, a yellow docket in one hand, blunt pencil in the other. He reached up and pulled nonchalantly on a length of twine that hung from a ceiling canister. As if we both had all day to kill, he began humming to himself, pushed the twine laboriously through the eyehole in the docket but did not attach it to the shoe.

'What do you mean Tommy?' I said.

'The name, what'll it be, will it be his or your own or what?'

I was flummoxed.

'Just put Anne Marie,' I said.

'No can do, no can do, no siree.' He shoved the pencil over his ear, sending raggy brown hair jutting outwards and with arms across the chest, he smiled beguilingly up at me, tapped the pencil on the workbench and waited.

'I don't know Tommy,' I said, a choke in my throat, my words in a wobble, 'I don't know what name I'll give you, I just don't know Tommy.'

'Lave it so,' he said, 'it's fine, fine, it's okay, I'll just put them down to your father.'

At a bank training course in Dublin, at the coffee break, a nice man asked if I was married or single.

'It's complicated,' I exhaled.

'Really, how could it be, simple yes or no I'd have thought, a yay or a nay as the fella says?'

'Well, it's not as simple as that. You see, I was married but I'm not anymore, so I'm technically single.'

'Technically?'

'Yeah, technically, but as I said it's complicated. Let's just say I am a recently separated, married woman, who's desperately trying to find a new way of describing myself.'

Fast forward four years when I met the love of my life and we moved to California, where I never needed an electric blanket. Name-changing was no game changer and divorce was practically commonplace. And in Ireland with a skin-of-the-teeth margin of 50.28 to 49.72 per cent the divorce referendum, which had previously failed, was won, the amendment to our constitution finally carried and signed into law on 27 November 1996. One of the stip-

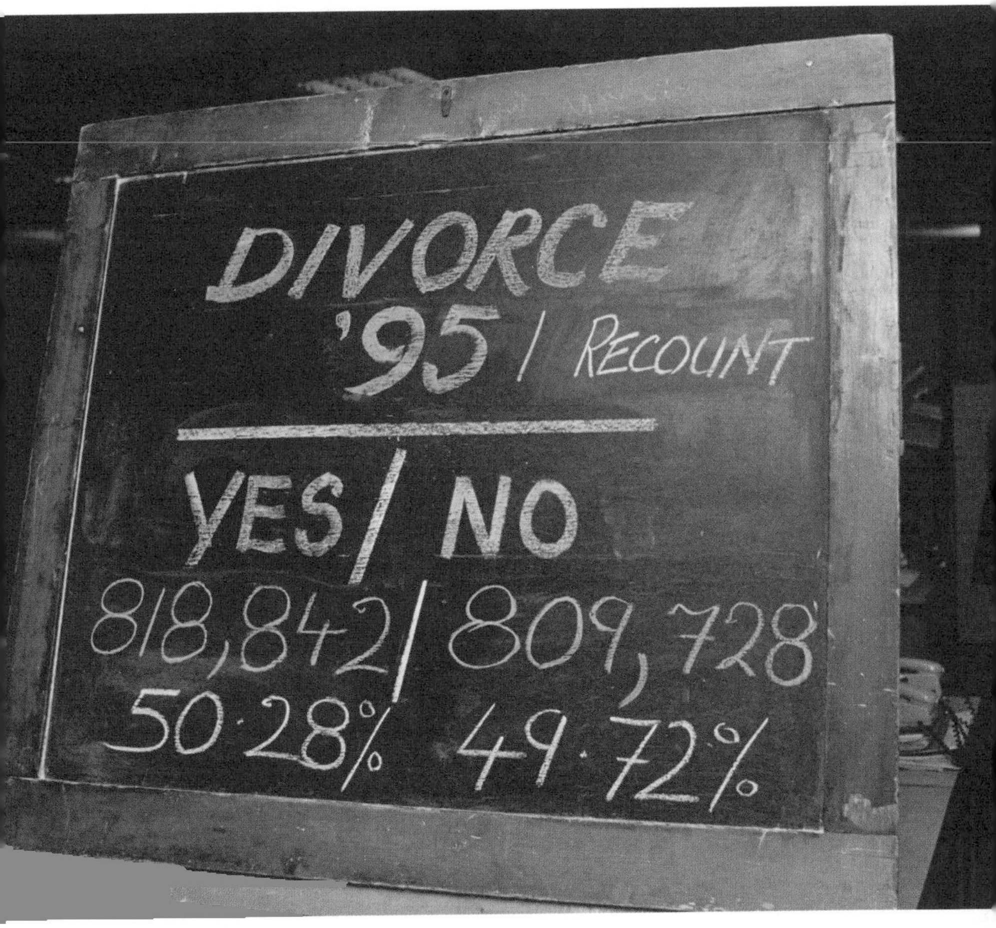
DIVORCE
'95 / RECOUNT
YES / NO
818,842 / 809,728
50·28% 49·72%

ulations was that the couple had to have lived apart for at least four years. I was slowly starting to tick the right boxes. My uneventful divorce process was completed, the legal paperwork stamped and twenty-two years ago I changed to my present name. We've come a long way in Ireland since 1991, but I will always remember it as a pivotal year in my life, having overcome and not succumbed to the mind-numbing administrative, cultural and legal inadequacies of a pre-divorce society. Nowadays, as a writer I am grateful for the material and memories those times inspire. As a performer I say my name frequently in public and I revel in the sound of it, my eponymous website announces me with it, I like being newly introduced by it.

And I am acutely aware of how much more there is to it than just a three-word series of letters. My name is my word, my reputation, my profile and countenance, it is my unique identifier and something I will never, ever take for granted.

The Origami of Girlhood

Sinéad Gleeson

1992 was the year of vectors, scalars, sine cos tan; plate tectonics. Charles Stuart Parnell. The *Módh Coinníollach*. The year of 'rollrock highroad roaring down'. The world was expanding, opening its folds – a vast origami, in all directions.

It was the year that childhood gave way to adulthood as I turned eighteen, moving from one to the other with a mix of thrill and unease. All of a sudden, I had the right to vote, drink and give blood.

Only two of those things mattered that summer. I was, at this point, a decade away from an illness that required many blood transfusions, years away from responsibility, from doing my taxes, caring about cholesterol, and from the constant, but pleasant, white noise that children are. That summer, I may not have cared much for blood, but I was vampiric. Black-clad, pale-skinned, at parties I commandeered the stereo to forcibly blare Kate Bush or The Pixies with Wagnerian gusto. I guarded the sound system like a sentry. I haunted basement bars and grotty venues to see bands of all stripes. Places that now wouldn't pass the most basic of fire and safety drills, but are singed into my memory. Where collective sweat dripped from the ceiling as crowds swayed in one heaving murmuration.

At one particular 1992 gig, I was in the front row. Squashed against the barriers in Dublin's SFX, someone's knuckles in my back, trying to avoid the lighted tips of other people's cigarettes. Nick Cave stood on the monitor, his vintage pimp shoes see-sawing back and forth, an apocalyptic preacher, stick-thin and raving. Outside, before the show, I waited for hours and he posed for a photo, taken by my first boyfriend. In it, there is a cigarette, clutched like a shiv

between my fingers – I had to guillotine off the lower half of the frame, so my parents wouldn't see it.

Another gig: in the smoky crypt of the Baggot Inn, Henry Rollins performed a spoken-word show. Rollins swooped down on his subject matter, landing on politics and art, uniting the women in the audience by dissing sexism. He extinguished every laugh by ending on a gut-punch story of how his best friend had been shot right in front of him only weeks before. This night was the first one I ever spent with that boyfriend. In his parents' bedroom I remember pink flowers on every surface. From wallpaper to carpet, it was an acid trip made of roses, a stockade of wild blooms.

We spent the summer in London, in a flat in Kentish Town with a Greek landlord who, baffled at our vegetarianism, made us stuffed vine leaves and spanakopita. We lived frugally, occasionally buying the odd £1.99 bottle of Liebfraumilch in Sainsbury's. One night before dinner I put it in the freezer to chill and forgot about it. The glass broke, and desperate to save the contents, I placed the bottle-shaped ice pop in a sieve over a pot on the cooker.

In 1992, because of said boyfriend, there were urgent admonishments from my mother about not getting pregnant. Poised as I was on the doorstep of life, her warnings were incantations, morality tales of clipped wings and receding horizons. I do not remember my brothers being warned about similar things.

In 1992 another girl, who wasn't yet a woman, got pregnant. The X case loomed, a modern horror story, a private whisper that became a public shout. It was the first time I was eligible to vote, on the life of a stranger who was only four years younger than me.

Across the water, the Church of England allowed women to become priests for the first time. Across the Atlantic, Sinéad O'Connor appeared on television singing Bob Marley's 'War' a cappella. Staring down the lens of the camera as though a gun, she tore up a picture of the Pope, declaring, 'Fight the real enemy!'

1992 was a bad year to be a fourteen-year-old girl or an outspoken singer, a worse year for autonomy and empathy, but it was a good year for speaking up, a good year for love.

After the summer the compass twitched, and from the Piccadilly and Northern lines I was Cinderella'd back to Dublin, broke and uncertain, sewing a black net bustle onto my debs skirt, which I wore – to my mother's horror – with a black basque and fishnets. The year shook itself out, stretched its limbs, and I was where I wanted to be – possibilities beating in my chest like a drum.

A Month of Poems

Enda Wyley

How can we ever know when our lives are going to change? Certainly, twenty-five years ago, struggling with my heavy old manual typewriter, as I arrived in Dún Laoghaire off the ferry from Holyhead, it was hard to feel that anything in my life would change. It was 1993. I was twenty-seven years old, exhausted and lonely, having left my life and friends behind in the North of England.

In those days there was no such thing as a master's in creative writing in Ireland and so I'd applied to Lancaster University and happily accepted a place there. I imagined days spent trailing the mudflats of Morecambe Bay, weekends exploring the Forest of Bowland, or the Yorkshire Dales, being inspired to write.

But writing a new poem each week for workshops proved hard work. And I mostly spent my days in the tiny attic room of the graduate building where I lived, clickety-clacketing new poems on my typewriter. If the skylight window was open, the sound would float out across the grass slopes and concrete paths of campus. One night I heard a group of students walking by below. 'That's that mad Irish girl typing,' one of them said. What would they have said if they'd known that I was typing poems? But I didn't care. I far preferred my typewriter over their 1990s computers – loved the thrill of the bell ringing at the end of each line, loved the press of the carriage return speeding me on.

Those months in Lancaster were times of intense reading and imagining. I read about the famous Pendle Witch trials of 1612, became convinced that the wronged women darkened the canal nearby when I walked there alone, heard their cackles in the undergrowth. Of course, these eerie thoughts were the stuff of new poems, as were my readings of poets I came to obsess over and write about. The dying Raymond Carver staring each day at a painting of salmon leaping upstream. Anna Akhmatova whispering poems to women outside Leningrad prison in 1940. Or Elizabeth Bishop, her bus suddenly stopped because a creature had blocked the road. Even now, craning back in time, I can see that majestic moose emerge from the impenetrable New Brunswick woods.

And now, it was 1993 and I was home, hauling my suitcase and that heavy typewriter out of the ferry, half crying from the weight of it all and stumbling into . . . what? I wasn't sure. But miraculously Dublin embraced me, welcomed me back. I found a house to live in with a friend, a school to teach in right in the heart of the city.

And no sooner had I returned than two famous poets visited the city. Allen Ginsberg was lured to Ireland for the first time in 1993 and read at Liberty Hall, much to the excitement of the hordes of people who flocked to see him. His payment was a fine Donegal tweed suit, purchased by then Poetry Ireland director Theo Dorgan, who discovered that Kevin & Howlin tailors on Nassau Street did a variation on the thornproof tweed that Ginsberg so desired. The irony of the tailor's name was not lost on Ginsberg himself, creator of the legendary poetry collection *Howl*.

Three years later, on his seventieth birthday in June 1996, a photographic self-portrait shows Ginsberg in the thornproof tweed suit made for him in Dublin. Since then, he'd only ever taken it off to be dry-cleaned and it was the very suit that he was laid out in when he died in April 1997 – the beat poet Gregory Corso, singer-songwriter Patti Smith and others coming to pay their respects.

That weekend in October 1993 when Ginsberg read – I still prize the yellow, faded ticket on my desk – the outstanding Czech poet Miroslav Holub also arrived in Dublin to read at the Irish Writers Centre.

The city buzzed with literary excitement, October 1993 proving to be a month of poets and poems. At the end of that month my first book of poems, developed in Lancaster and finally completed in Dublin, was published. And though it often ended up in the cookery section in bookshops because of its title, *Eating Baby Jesus*, I remember feeling that something was changing. I had stepped off the ferry from England uncertain as to where I was going, or what might happen. But now the weight of that old typewriter had been eased from me, my hands spreading out to new possibilities. Like Holub's poem, a door was opening. And I knew that even if there was nothing there, at least there'd be a draught.

Proof

Claire Kilroy

In 1994 I went to New York on my own to work for the summer. I wasn't supposed to go on my own. I was supposed to go with my friend, but she bailed shortly before we were due to leave because she couldn't cobble together the air fare. So, with something to prove, off I went. I was twenty.

I found an apartment by answering an ad in a laundrette. It was a one bed in Alphabet City, back when *A* was for *Assault*, *B* was for *Battery*, *C* was for *Crime* and *D* was for *Death*. I lived on *D*. I was taking the room of a guy who was heading off for the summer, he explained through an unwavering smile. The other inhabitant of the apartment, a kind fellow with an unfortunate surname who worked nights as a doorman, slept during the day on the couch outside my room. The two guys hot-bunked on the doorman's couch when flatmate *uimhir a haon* arrived back two months early. 'I'm off heroin!' he announced, still beaming.

I spent the summer attending AA meetings, not because I was a recovering alcoholic but because I fell in with a group of them. The stories I heard. I had no frame of reference for the abyss these people lived on the brink of. I had not understood that there was an abyss, that an entire life could be spent hovering just one drink away from it.

I got fired from six waitressing jobs in a row, having never waitressed before, having barely eaten in restaurants before. The game was up: I was out of money. Then I somehow got a job in the Empire State Building working on the 86th-floor observatory, folding T-shirts and selling tat. We peeled the *Made in China* stickers off Big Apples and Statues of Liberty and displayed them on shelves. Some random details that I recall: Japanese tourists gasping in horror when one of their video cameras shattered across the tiled floor; our manager screaming at closing time that OJ was innocent; the pleasure that Bo, the elevator operator, took from loading tourists into his descending metal box and then, as the doors slid shut, calling out 'Lemmings!'

When I was leaving, the flatmate with the unfortunate surname – whom I just googled to discover is now a magician – gave me a card and a gift. The card said he was sorry I had had such a hard time, and that the gift was to remind me of how I felt in New York. It was a keyring of Edvard Munch's *Scream*. From the smoking ruins of that summer – for there was more to it that I won't go into here – I plucked just one artefact, an object I always paused to admire whenever I was setting it out for sale: a pewter magnet of the Empire State Building. Unlike everything else on the stall, it was solid, well wrought and possessed of a certain heft that reflected the art deco glory of the building it was designed to commemorate.

Fifteen years later and I was looking for The One. How will I know you? I wondered, for he was a You, this person I had to locate among all the other people. How will I know You are You?

When I first saw my husband, I recognised him. It was the strangest thing. I had never met this man before, but I looked into his eyes and I knew him. Then he started doing *Terminator* impressions and morphed back into Some Bloke. This isn't working, I told him after the second date.

He promised not to do any more *Terminator* impressions and negotiated a third date. After dinner we ended up careening around town on a pair of Dublin Bikes. I hadn't been on a bike since childhood and couldn't stop laughing.

I cannot remember at what point I saw my Empire State Building magnet on his fridge and wondered how it had gotten there, or maybe he saw his Empire State Building magnet on my fridge and wondered the same, until we established that we had both been to

New York during the mid-90s and, out of the vast ocean of souvenirs on sale, and despite neither of us being the kind of people who bought souvenirs, we had both alighted upon this one and brought it home, and carried it with us to the many homes we had separately inhabited during the intervening years, like the missing half of a broken-heart locket from a Victorian novel, which, when finally reunited with the other half, confirms, in that miraculous moment when the jagged edges connect, that this indeed is the person we have been seeking, that we have finally found one another, that here is further proof.

Microphone

Rosaleen McDonagh

They say activists are born rather than made. But for me, I trace my formation as an activist from a terrifying experience in my childhood, all the way to the first time I spoke into a microphone and people listened.

Growing up, whenever there was a programme on television about African-American people looking for equal rights, I was all ears. On hearing of apartheid in South Africa my heart too would quicken its pace. I felt an instinctive affinity with these people, a shared history. But I hadn't yet started to put it all together.

Me and my sisters were inducted young into Traveller feminism, though. The older *beoirs* often lacked formal education but the wisdom and knowledge they passed on to us could not be matched by a certificate or a degree from college. They could articulate the problems of sexism and racism in a brash and bold way. Traveller women have been the custodians of our culture and the biggest influence in my life. They are the negotiators, the peacemakers, the advocates, the ones who have cradled our resistance and representation.

My family moved from Sligo to Dublin when I was eleven. We joined other families who were living on the Tallaght bypass. As children we did not know or understand the hostility towards us. We thought settled people were strange and that they were living their lives the wrong way. One day myself and my sister Jules, who was only a toddler, were playing in our trailer. My father, along with other men, was standing and acting very nervous halfway down the road of trailers. My mother was out hanging the clothes on the washing line.

Suddenly, we heard a commotion and stopped our game. We both climbed up onto the bunk in the trailer to look out the window. There was a crowd of settled men shouting 'Travellers out!' As they moved closer toward the trailer it became more frightening. Then they started rattling and rocking the trailer. Grabbing my little sister, I lay on the floor with her so they couldn't see us. She crawled under me with fear.

Amidst all the chaos I manage to climb back onto the bunk and looked out the window, searching for a familiar face. To the left the *beoirs,* including my mother, were running towards us and telling the men who were shaking our trailer that there were children playing inside. Baby Jules was hysterical but over all the noise, my mother's screams were the loudest. The men pushed and pushed and our home was turned over onto the ground. With the fall of the trailer the windows were in smithereens. Shards of glass came in on top of us. In our hair and in our clothes. I heard the sound of my mother's delph and other ornaments breaking into pieces.

At the back of the trailer a gas bottle had been rigged up underneath the window. The nozzle had come off with all the commotion. The smell was so strong. For a moment, there was an eerie quiet. Everything seemed calm. The men seemed all at once to realise what they had done; we heard them running away. Blood was running down my baby sister's face. A hand came in through the window. It was a young garda. He was shaking. He grabbed us both and pulled us out. We all fell on the ground, and with my little sister in my arms, I watched our home go up in flames.

Spring 1995. I was a grown woman, happy and confident. Pavee Point, the pioneering Traveller centre, was going to mark its tenth anniversary. There was a shindig to celebrate and I had been asked to speak.

For many of us Traveller girls growing up, it was Pavee Point who offered us our first educational opportunities. Our expectations were raised; our ambitions were widened. Tradition was being pulled and stretched. We'd experienced racism, discrimination; now we would analyse it and learn from it. Traveller voices were emerging and everyone was beginning to realise that self-determination rather than assimilation was the only way forward.

On entry to Pavee Point that day, you could hear Margaret Barry's music being played. The smell of freshly baked soda bread held out the promise of a second breakfast for all of us. All over the building, people were rehearsing their poetry, songs and passionate polemical speeches. The media cameras were there. I found a quiet corner, and looked over my own speech. 'Women's rights are Travellers' rights,' it began.

That day in Pavee Point was the first time in my life that I was ever trusted with a microphone. My name was called. The room fell silent. The memory of our trailer in flames came burning back.

The voices of previous generations came out of my mouth, as I started to speak.

Year of the Conservatory

Éilís Ní Dhuibhne

A sunroom, like a greenhouse, leans against the back wall of our house, looking out on the garden full of shrubs, the huge pink rhododendrons in full bloom. It appeared two days ago. Over the weekend, I installed some wicker chairs, a small table, and the first plants – ferns for *ferniness*, geraniums for colour.

Naturally I believed I or we – although it was mostly I who desired things like a conservatory – were acting independently, making a free choice, to add this little glass room to our house. True, I'd been influenced by the Joneses. Our next-door neighbour had had one for a while, and I had always envied her it. I could see several, glittering on the backs of houses, as I travelled in and out of Dublin on the Dart to work every day. (The Dart is great for allowing you to see into other people's back gardens, their private space, as they think.)

A good friend in Bray had just got one – in fact, I got the name of the man who put them up, from her. But I didn't know I was part of history, as I rang this man up and got a quote and waited and waited and waited until he arrived one day out of the blue, like a messenger from the skies, and performed the miracle. I didn't know that half the country was getting a conservatory, in 1996.

My sunroom was not an event of any historical importance, was it? History was happening in other places – for instance, up the road, in the North of Ireland. But down here, smaller, more nuanced, less significant historical change was underway. The economy was changing. For the first time since I had got married fourteen years earlier, we had enough spare money to buy the conservatory. Five thousand pounds – we were still on pounds. It seemed to me we had the money because I had written a play and had it produced in 1995, and by 1996 I was getting some prizes, for the play and for other things – people were ringing me up, asking me to write things, sometimes telling me I had won a prize. Was that historical? Yes, it was. They were asking me to do these things because I was a woman. Women writers, who had been largely ignored or reviled for centuries, were in fashion.

In 1996 for the first time we had a bank statement which wasn't in the red. In those days you got your bank statement once a month in the post, a list of figures in black and red. The red was the amount by which you were overdrawn. For fourteen years we had been permanently overdrawn – just paying the normal bills had kept us in the red right through the 1980s and into the middle of the 90s. And we were a middle-class couple with two quite well-paid jobs – the lucky ones.

Now in 1996 we were no longer in the red. Not because much was changing in the way we ran our lives. We just started getting more money for doing what we'd been doing all along – teaching, librarianing, writing. The change had nothing to do with us, with successful writing or better research or more efficient thriftiness. It happened because the Celtic Tiger was starting.

For the next ten years or so, Ireland was going to be a good place to live for me and my family, and for a lot of people. There would be jobs. There would be travel. There would be cappuccinos and wine at weekends. There would be Ryanair and holidays abroad and weekend breaks. Emigration would slow down, stop, and the miracle of immigration – who could have imagined it – would become a feature of life. In 1996 people turned to stare at you if you spoke a language that wasn't English, on the Dart – even when that language was Irish. Ten years on, trying to identify the myriad languages I could hear at any time on the Dart became one of my hobbies.

I learned to figure that if they said *da* a lot and *shh sh* it was something Slavonic, if they sang up and down it was some sort of

Chinese – I still kept a close eye on the eternally fascinating back gardens and what was going on in them, which was, usually, extensions. Towards the end of the Celtic Tiger all the conservatories were torn down and replaced by big extensions with proper roofs.

We didn't have mobile phones. There were 140,000 of them in Ireland in 1996. The cheapest models cost a hundred pounds. Calls on the Eircell network (possibly the only one) cost 21p per minute at off-peak times and 30p per minute otherwise, plus a connection fee and 18 pounds a month rental. An *Irish Times* report says that the buyers of mobile phones in 1996 were predominantly male, although, since the latest models would be small enough to fit in a handbag, women were getting interested – apparently unless it could fit in a handbag women would ignore the modern technology. It was still OK to patronise women in *The Irish Times* in 1996. The internet was already in the country – well, in UCD and Trinity, for instance. But not in my home nor in most people's. We were still on the landline phone in the hall, and there was no email.

1996 was not just the year of the black bank account and the lean-to conservatory. Social and political change was also happening. Mary Robinson was President of Ireland, Bill Clinton President of the United States, George Mitchell had been appointed head of a commission to try to achieve a peaceful settlement in Northern Ireland. In 1995 the people of Ireland had voted to repeal the ban on divorce in this country and the right to divorce was signed into legislation in June 1996. It was the first of the referendums which liberalised life, pulled it out from under the tough laws of the Catholic bishops.

Yes. Yes. Yes.

The change was beginning.

1996. The year of the sunrooms. The year we started to lighten up.

Múnlaí Briste

Simon Ó Faoláin

Bhí an cóiméad Hale-Bopp dochreidte geal agus é i ngiorracht na gréine le linn earrach 1997, é romhat gach oíche idir Lá 'le Bríde agus Bealtaine, a ruball fada geal ar sileadh leis: sionnach bán ag fiach na réaltanna thar bhánta na spéire. Don té a ghéillfeadh do phiseoga seanbhunaithe i gcultúir éagsúla ar fud na cruinne, is comhartha é teacht cóiméid go bhfuil athrú ó bhonn ar na bacáin. Ainm eile orthu ná Réalta na Scuaibe, agus shamhlófaí gur ag úsáid na scuaibe sin a bhíonn siad chun an sean-rud a ghlanadh amach is an tslí a dhéanamh réidh don rud nua.

Chríochnaigh mise mo thráchtas seandálaíochta i 1997. Bhí trí bliana tugtha agam ag déanamh iniúchadh ar theicneolaíocht na gceardaithe miotail le linn na Cré-umhaoise. Bhí fiche bliain d'oiliúint curtha isteach agam ón mbunscoil ar aghaidh, agus mé anois ag fágaint slán le múnla an chórais oideachais fé dheireadh thiar. Ach ní raibh obair sheasta ar fáil sa chathair ná in aon áit eile, agus d'fhilleas abhaile ar Chorca Dhuibhne.

Le linn dom a bheith díomhaoin os comhair na teilifíse tráthnóna amháin, chonaic mé aghaidh theicneolaíocht úrnua á nochtadh don saol. Aghaidh neamhurchóideach chaorach a bhí ann a raibh ainm ag dul leis: Dolly. Í á tabhairt amach os comhair na ceamaraí teilifíse ar cheann téide ag eolaí, casóga bána orthu araon. Clón ab ea Dolly, déanta ina macasamhail foirfe de chaora eile, gan aon ghá le reithe. Tugadh le fios dúinn gur teicneolaíocht é seo a bhris monaplacht an ghnéis mar an t-aon bhealach giniúna leis na billiúin bliana. Cúis iontais agus mhíshuaimhnis.

Ag deireadh an fhómhair fuair mise conradh chun anailís a dhéanamh ar ábhar miotalóireachta a fuarthas ar thochailt seandálaíochta. Píosaí de mhúnlaí cré ab ea formhór an ábhair seo, iad briste ina smidiríní ag na ceardaithe chun scaoileadh a dhéanamh ar na huirlisí nó na hairm a deineadh iontu nuair a dhoirteadh an cré-umha leáite isteach iontu: tua, sleá, casúr, rásúr, claíomh. Is cúis iontais dom fós a bheith ag samhlú an nóiméad san nuair a dtógfaí suas an múnla – é torrach, é fós te ar nós buillín aráin ag teacht ón oighean – is go mbrisfí an chré gharbh bhácálta, ag nochtadh ghile an chré-umha – é cruaidh, mín, geal, lonnrach. Tré scoilt caol ar dtúis a bhfeicfí é, ansin níos mó agus níos mó go bhfeicfí an toradh iomlán. Míorúilt den teicneolaíocht nua-aimseartha a bhí sa ghnó seo ag an am. Ní mar sin a d'fhéach na gnáthdhaoine ceithre mhíle bliana ó shin ar an gceardaí miotail is a shaothair. Ní teicneolaíocht dóibh na claochluithe diamhra a bhain leis an obair seo. Draíocht a bhí ann dóibh, agus draoithe ab ea lucht a ndéanta.

I 1997 bhí go leor daoine ann a bhí míshásta le Dolly agus an clónáil seo. Dúirt na daoine seo go raibh na heolaithe ag iarraidh áit Dé a thógaint, rud a fhág gur saghas Agnus Dei ab ea Dolly, nó Agnus déithe bréige, ar a laghad. Dúradh go raibh na múnlaí á mbriseadh ag Dolly agus an saol athraithe ó bhonn. Ach má bhris sí múnlaí, chruthaigh sí múnlaí diamhra eile.

Pé scéal é, bhí na céadta píosaí de mhúnlaí cré – múnlaí nach raibh meafarach – le hiniúchadh agamsa, is gan saotharlann sa tigh againn, ná fiú seid lasmuigh. Ní raibh de rogha agam ach iad a leagadh amach im' sheomra leapan: ar an mbord, ar leic na fuinneoige, ar an tseilf, ar an leaba bhreise, agus fiú ar an úrlár (ach ag cinntiú go raibh cosán nocht chomh fada leis an steirió). Gach píosa ina luí ar a mhála beag féin ar a raibh uimhir fionnachtana agus fáisnéise eile fé scríofa. Bhínn ag obair orthu i rith an lae agus im' luí ina measc istoíche, mo leaba mar oileán ina lár.

Bhí an geimhreadh sin dorcha, fliuch, garbh, na gálaí ón Atlantach isteach ag sciúirseáil na leithinse mar is dual dóibh. Na hoícheanta doininne seo, ní chloisinn aon rud ach gaoth is fearthainn lasmuigh. Ach na oícheanta fhánacha a mbíodh sámhnas ann, do chloisinn na múnlaí tré mo thaibhrimh, iad ag cogarnach is ag siosarnach lena chéile, nó b'fhéidir liomsa. N'fheadar cad a bhíodh á rá acu, ach bhí blas na hársaíochta ar a bhfriotail.

As Béarla glaotar 'historicity' ar an gcumhacht a mbraitear ar an ní árss nuair a láimhseáiltear é, nó fiú nuair a fhéachtar air. Is cumhacht na samhlaíochta é seo, agus sinn ag iarraidh na féidearthachtaí a bhaineann le stair fhada an ní sin a shamhlú. Bhí cumhacht dhiamhar sna píosaí seo de mhúnlaí dar le muintir na Cré-umhaoise chomh maith, cumhacht chosanta. Chuirtí iad thairseacha tí, nó fé phollaí geata, in uaigheanna agus ar láithreacha naofa eile iad. Is ionann an chumhacht sa dá chás: 'historicity' an sean-rud dúinne inniu, agus cumhacht osnádúrtha na draíochta nua-aimseartha don nduine sa Chré-umhaois. Dúinne toisc é a bheith sean, dóibhsean toisc é a bheith nua.

Tá áthas orm a rá inniu nach bhfuil daoine éirithe as an gcomhriachtain sna fiche bliain ó deineadh clónáil ar Dolly. Agus maidir le Dolly féin, tá sí go diail. Cé go bhfuil sí imithe ar shlí na firinne, tá ceithre chlón foirfe di fós ar marthain inniu: Daisy, Debbie, Denise agus Dianna.

Broken Moulds

Simon Ó Faoláin

The comet Hale Bopp was incredibly bright as it neared the sun in spring 1997. Always there in your face every night between St Bridget's Day and *Bealtaine*, its long shining tail flowing away behind: a white fox hunting the stars across the sky's fields. For those who incline to superstition, the approach of a comet is a sign that great change is coming. Another Irish name for them is *Réalta na Scuaibe* (the star of the brush), and one might imagine that brush being used to sweep out the old and clear the way for the new.

I completed my archaeology thesis in 1997. I had spent three years researching the Bronze Age metalworker's craft. Having spent twenty years in education from primary school onwards, I was finally departing the mould of the education system. But there was no steady work to be found in the city or anywhere else, and I returned home to Corca Dhuibhne.

There, on the television one evening, I saw a new technology being revealed to the world. It had the harmless face of a sheep: Dolly was her name. She was led out on a rope before the television cameras by a scientist, both of them wearing a white coat. Dolly was a clone, made as a perfect replica of another sheep, with no need for the involvement of a ram. We were informed that this was a technology, which meant that sex would shortly be superseded as a means of procreation. A cause for wonder and uneasiness.

At the end of autumn I was given a contract to carry out analysis on metallurgical material from an archaeological excavation. Most of this consisted of fragments of moulds, which had been smashed to smithereens to reveal the tools or weapons formed when molten bronze was poured into them: axes, spears, hammers, razors, swords. It excites me still to imagine the moment when the mould was taken in the hand – pregnant, still hot like a loaf of bread straight out of the oven – and the rough, baked clay was broken, revealing the bronze within – hard, smooth, bright and shining. Through a narrow crack it would first be seen, then more and more until the entire product was exposed. This process was a miracle of modern technology in its time. But that is not how ordinary people four thousand years ago regarded the metalworker and his craft. For them, the supernatural transformations involved were not technology, but sorcery, and those who practised them, sorcerers.

In 1997 there were many people who were unhappy about Dolly and this new cloning. These people said that the scientists were 'playing God', something that implies that Dolly must have been a sort of Agnus Dei – Lamb of God, or Lamb of False Gods at least. It was also said that Dolly had broken the mould and that life was irreversibly changed. But if she broke moulds, she also formed other ones.

Anyway, I had hundreds of pieces of clay moulds – which were in no way metaphorical – to examine, and we lacked a laboratory in the house. There was no choice but to lay them out in my bedroom: on the table, the windowsill, the shelves, the spare bed, and even the floor. Each fragment lying on its own little bag on which was written the find number and other information. I would work on them in the daytime and lie among them at night, my bed an island in their midst.

That winter was dark, wet and rough, the gales in from the Atlantic scourging the peninsula as was their wont. Those nights I would hear nothing but wind and rain outside. But the occasional night when all was still, I would hear the moulds in my dreams, whispering and hissing among themselves. I could not tell what they were saying, but their chatter had a distinctly ancient accent. In English the term 'historicity' is sometimes used for the power we perceive in an ancient thing when we handle it or even look at it. This is an imaginative power, as we try to imagine the possibilities inherent in the object's long history. There was power in these mould fragments for Bronze Age people also, protective power. They laid them under the thresholds or the gateposts of their houses. The two powers are the same: the historicity of an ancient object for us today, and the power of the new magic for the person in the Bronze Age. For us, because it is old; for them, because it was new.

1998 came and I went abroad excavating in Portugal, leaving darkness, storms and the whispering of the moulds behind me. Twenty years later, I am glad to say people have not given up sex out of preference for cloning. As regards Dolly, although she has passed away, her mould has survived: four perfect copies of her are living today: Daisy, Debbie, Denise and Dianna. The Queen is dead, long live the Queen!

IV
1998–2007

Setting the Scene

Colin Murphy

Between the years of 1998 and 2007 I lived in eighteen houses, in eight towns, in four countries, in two continents. So I find those garda vetting forms, where they ask for *previous addresses since birth*, a little complicated.

In 1998, freshly graduated, two of my friends had so-called 'good jobs' in Ireland: one in the bank, the other in a bookshop. The rest of us had left. We'd grown up in the 1980s; that was what we knew.

The surprise was that, soon, people started coming home. Word was there was *work*: actor friends were coming off the dole to get work in IT call centres, alongside French and Spanish kids who'd moved to Dublin to answer phones in French and Spanish to customers in France and Spain. (In the era of the reverse-charge, long-distance phone call, that made *no* sense.)

I had gone the other way, moving to Madrid to test myself. After twenty-three years in Dublin 4, I thought it was maybe time to broaden my horizons. And I found that I liked the heat, liked being surrounded by a foreign language, liked the vibrancy of their culture, liked the hustle of their city, liked fending for myself. It gave life an edge. I didn't want to come home. I wanted to test myself further.

In February 2000 I landed in Luanda, Angola, a city that seemed like it had been evacuated mid-construction by the Portuguese in 1975 and was still unfinished. Within two weeks of arriving, I was on my back with malaria. I buckled.

'You've taken a knock,' said my boss. 'Everybody takes a knock.'

I thought I couldn't cope – that I had failed. I nearly came home. But this was the test I had wanted.

I stayed. I learned how to get things done, how to deal with soldiers, how to dance. But after two years, I was emotionally exhausted – or, perhaps, desiccated. I needed to move on but wasn't ready to come home.

I moved to Johannesburg, to study. But the surprise was that Johannesburg was harder than Angola: Angola was a hostile environment, but the people were warm; Johannesburg, a Western-style city, was a familiar environment, but the people were hostile.

But, gradually, like Angola, and like Madrid before it, Johannesburg sucked me in. I adjusted to its rhythms and learned its ways. I liked the edge.

I didn't plan to move back to Ireland. I didn't know what I would do, here. But there was a girl, here, and I came back to woo her and persuade her to move abroad with me.

The surprise was that, whatever about me, she wasn't convinced of the attractions of Johannesburg. The wooing happened; the persuasion didn't. Without quite realising it, I was home.

It wasn't until about eighteen months later that I realised I was depressed. It took a doctor to point it out, after I'd gone to him in the wake of a three-in-the-morning panic attack. I was referred to a counsellor, a trauma specialist, but he wanted to talk about what I'd seen in Angola – poverty, famine, violence, death. I didn't want to talk about that, unless I was trading blackly-comic stories with other aid workers.

And it wasn't that I was suffering the trauma of the contrast between the world I had been in and the world of ostentation and opulence that Dublin was becoming. I wasn't particularly interested in our new-found wealth, but nor was I interested in judging it. So I wasn't haunted by my experience abroad – I missed it. I had felt a purpose. It was the edge that gave life definition. Now, trying to get a foothold in a career and life in Dublin, I felt like I was faking it.

I don't know if I realised that at the time. I schlepped out to Dún Laoghaire once a week to talk to a therapist, an interesting and thoughtful man to whom I didn't really want to be talking because I didn't know what to say. I didn't know what I felt.

Much of my life was good: I found a tiny cottage with my girl-friend and, with deep breaths, we signed a 35-year mortgage. But even with that anchor, I was still unmoored. By the end of this decade I had tried English teaching, academia, aid work, broadcasting, freelance journalism and playwriting – which reads like the CV of someone resolutely determined to avoid the Celtic Tiger. I had spent ten years searching. I had found versions of myself, but they didn't feel whole. I had left parts of myself in other places.

And then, at another three in the morning, at the end of that decade, we left our tiny cottage and drove down the hill to the Rotunda and arrived back eight hours later with a daughter. And all the adventures, and all the tests, and all the searching, and all the trauma of the previous decade was irrelevant. Because the biggest test, the hardest adventure, the greatest trauma was just starting.

But the surprise was that I was finally moored. And in the decade since, I've lived in one house.

A home.

The Crest of a Wave

John MacKenna

From a long time ago and a great distance away, names and faces find their way back through the emptying stadiums of memory.

Ask me about the spring or the early summer of 1998 and I'll tell you I remember very little. I moved house, planted a new garden, built drystone walls and travelled to see Kildare play Dublin in the Leinster Senior Football quarter-final. Travelled as I had done for forty years, as Kildare supporters always do, with faith but without certainty; with insecurity but not entirely devoid of hope. That strange coagulation of the footballing blood that is part of our DNA.

The previous year had been a case of almost but not quite. A thirteen-man Kildare, managed by Mick O'Dwyer, had beaten Laois and taken Meath to two replays before going down, so none of us knew what the new season might hold.

On the first Sunday in June 1998, we drew with Dublin. It looked as though we might never get across the starting line, let alone the finishing line. Forty-two years without a Leinster title stretched behind us like an empty road on a winter evening. Two weeks later we were back in Croke Park and nosed home by a point in a game that was tense to the bitter end.

Four weeks would pass before we faced Laois on the same pitch – these were the days when there were no back doors. You went through the front door of victory or you stayed away. This time we strolled home: 2 goals, 13–8 winners. And suddenly it was the first Sunday in August and there were the Lilywhites running out onto Croke Park to face Meath in a Leinster final.

My memories of that afternoon are that we seemed to have it won but Meath — as ever — refused to lie down and suddenly the dream was enveloped in the shadows of a nightmare. Trevor Giles and Tommy Dowd and Jody Devine took their points and it looked as though the 42-year wait would stretch to at least another year. And then it happened — Brian Murphy took a pass from Martin Lynch in the dying minutes and drove it past the Meath defence and into the Hill 16 goal. When the final whistle sounded, we had won by five points and the stands drained like a ruptured milk tanker and a wash of white flooded across the pitch and Glen Ryan sang 'The Curragh of Kildare' and there among the crowd of faces was Dermot Earley Senior, who had managed Kildare before Mick O'Dwyer's second coming, and we shook hands and I thanked him for the work he'd put in and the wave of white rolled back and forth across the pitch and the sun was dipping before we hit the Naas Road, still euphoric, still not quite believing.

Four weeks later we were back in Croke Park, beating Kerry by a point, reaching an All-Ireland Final, which now filled our every waking and sleeping moment.

The last Sunday in September dawned grey and overcast. I was on crutches. The night before my son, Ewan, and myself had played the match on the lawn — a season-long tradition — and I had torn ligaments in fielding a high ball. I should have read the omens but we were going into the game having beaten the 1995, '96 and '97 champions en route so even I, the eternal pessimist, had hope.

The match itself is something I still shudder to remember. There was the injury that Glen Ryan carried onto the field; there was the wonderful but ultimately false dawn of the first half; there was Dermot Earley's goal, which gave us a three-point half-time lead; there was Pádraic Joyce's goal that put the Tribesmen back in control and, from there to the end, try as Kildare might, we couldn't catch them. The final whistle saw Galway clear by four and suddenly the seats around us were empty as their supporters streamed down the aisles and onto the pitch.

Ewan sat hunched beside me, unable to speak, his body convulsing in spasms of tears and desolation. I was no better. I had dared to believe, as the summer grew into autumn, that the unimaginable might happen, that the seventy-year wait for an All-Ireland might end.

And then I saw an elderly Galway man, who had been making his way down the steps towards the pitch, stop and watch us for a moment before slowly climbing back up and edging along the row of seats until he stood behind us. Gently he placed a big, work-hardened hand on each of our shoulders, leaned over and said, very quietly: 'Always, always be proud of your county.'

From a long time ago and a great distance away, names and faces and voices find their way back through the deserted stadiums of memory and his is one of the clearest.

Ready for 2000

Honor Clynes

Luddite, technophobe, grumpy old (or middle-aged) woman, con-scientious objector to matters technological. Of all the above mon-ikers, I like the sound of Luddite best, though I'm not actually aggressively opposed to technological advances; it's just that, as one might say about, for example, sky-diving: 'It's just not for me.'

I have a mobile phone; I'm actually quite attached to it, mainly because my Nokia is exactly that – a portable device for making/receiving calls and writing/reading short messages. Because of pres-sure from just about everybody I also have a hand-held computer, also known as a 'smart' phone, but my transition period from the stupid to the clever phone has been a rather lengthy process. I do use a laptop, send and receive emails and occasionally google (a verb, I note, having consulted said Professor Google, which entered the Oxford Dictionary in 2006). However, I suppose I must admit to a partiality for looking back rather than forward: I enjoyed flicking through the index cards in the little drawers in libraries to find the name of an author or the classification of a book, until the boxes were wrested from me and replaced by, horror of horrors, an *e-resource*.

Back in the 1980s a friend and I decided, on a whim, to have dinner in a restaurant. As this meant that I wasn't returning home for my mother's dinner, naturally I had to phone her, so I asked the waiter if they had a phone I could use and, rather than leading me to a payphone with button A and B in a pokey cubbyhole, he brought out – wait for it – a phone on a very long line. We were so highly amused by this that I was barely able to impart the message to my bewildered mother and it definitely defined our evening. This was my first encounter with a portable phone (mobile phones were still in the distance).

I am not quite alone. A fellow Luddite soulmate of mine had her first introduction to an intercom as she rang the doorbell at a doctor's door in Fitzwilliam Square only to be asked by a disembodied voice who was there. Looking around in a befuddled and embarrassed manner she eventually whispered to the door handle, 'It's me!'

The history of the ATM (automated teller machine) in Ireland mirrors *Sunday Miscellany's* almost exactly, marking the fiftieth anniversary of its arrival in 2017. That said, it must be acknowledged that, while it might have been handy to go to the hole in the wall, it wasn't by any means essential because, until recently, banks actually *welcomed* customers across the threshold, although their opening hours were challenging. Interestingly, although Japan was at the forefront in the development of ATMs, then known as computer loan machines, in 1966 ATMs were not at all common in Japan, which stubbornly – to my delight – remains a cash society.

Anyway, I'm proud to have managed to reach the year 1999 without using an ATM, and although I had a PIN, I never bothered memorising it and made a personal commitment never to use one. Then a friend of mine became ill – not seriously, but just enough to keep her housebound and without cash for a few weeks. So she asked me to do her a favour. Obviously, she had no idea what she was asking of me! Could I take her card, memorise her PIN and go to the ATM in the local supermarket and withdraw £200 from her account? It would have been too foolhardy to show bravado and pretend to know what to do, so I had to admit I hadn't a clue. She patiently took me through the procedure, describing vividly and accurately what would appear on screen and what buttons I would push.

Many rehearsals later, I went to the supermarket and approached the machine. I was in a lather of sweat as this wasn't even my money, with her card in one hand and her PIN scribbled on a piece of paper in the other. Everything came up on screen, exactly as she had described. As she wanted £200, I had to punch in £200.00, otherwise I might get £20 or £2. All going well, perspiration reducing, I even looked nonchalantly around, hoping someone I knew would spot my technological prowess. Just as the machine started to spew out the cash a notice appeared on the screen: *Ready for £2000.*

£2000? £2000! Oh no! I actually started trying to stuff the notes back into the machine but was hampered by my sweaty hands. Another frantic look at the screen and I realised that there wasn't a £ sign in front of the 2000. This was 1999, and this bank machine, unlike its user, was ready for 2000.

A Space Odyssey

Stephen James Smith

Now and then I look back,
To think about then and now.
Now and then I wonder,
How I got here somehow ...

Then I was half my current age,
Now I'm not twice the person.
Yet there's reason to turn the page,
As all the regret will worsen.

If failure is as frightening
As what could be.
What will be, will be ...

I look back to me at the turn of
The century, the Millennium.
It was the year I'd to cast off
Childish ways to join my fellow men.

After the X Generation,
Millennial snowflakes decoration
Adorned the definition to
Discard the context of the past.
It was all ahead of me then,
It always will be I know now ...

I rang in the New Year with friends
In Enniskerry in a barn,
We broke into a boarding school
To sleep, but I'll spare you that yarn!

The Y2K bug fooled us all,
And alas we all sang goodbye
To Frank Patterson and the
Intoxicating Liquor Act passed
As an unholy hour
Began to signal a waning power . . .

As Pope John Paul II says sorry,
A PlayStation 2 sets the masses free!
As the twenty-first century begins,
Putin is the Russian president.
Clinton visits us to give a Northern Ireland address,
while Hillary is the first First Lady to win public office.

And the fat cats are still grinning,
Some things never change, the one per cent keeps winning.
And how now mad cow as the saying goes,
The BSE outbreak added to farming woes.

We had a century leap year,
366 days of growing fear
Causing the dotcom bubble burst!
While the public began to thirst
For voyeuristic ways *Big Brother*
Was broadcast bringing us back to 1984 days.
But *let's all meet up in the year 2000 . . .*
Won't it be strange when we're all fully grown . . .
We can reminisce on what we all miss
Be it a first kiss, listening to the wireless,
Or celebrating going cordless
With your phone and blasting out the polyphonic ringtones
Like a 'Crazy Frog' while playing Sonic the Hedgehog . . .

We've come from LimeWire to Spotify,
Then I remember slow dial-up connections,
MySpace and Encarta.
Now it's all 'What's your Wi-Fi code?'
Wikipedia and 'Add me on Insta!'

Then it was all floppy disks, Golden Discs and searching the
Yellow Pages,
Now it's all solid state, Bluetooth and liking Facebook pages.
Then it was Teletext, VHS or Betamax.
Now we've predictive text, as Netflix 'n' chill reaches a climax!

Now I've
Gained weight
Lost friends
Found perspective
Forgot birthdays
Unearthed truths
Cursed suicides
Discovered depression
Reclaimed hope!

And who knows what the future holds for us,
A 2.4 family, some more fuss . . .

We can't know where we're going,
'till we've seen where we've been.
And yet all thoughts are of the present,
and in the present it seems . . .

Now and then I look back
To think about then and now.
Now and then I wonder
How we got here somehow.

Be the Change

Barbara Scully

Mia, my youngest daughter, is a music-obsessed, art-mad, eighteen-year-old hippie. Her bedroom looks like something that the 1970s left behind, with the dark purple walls adorned with batik hangings, photos of her favourite bands and her own swirling, groovy artwork. Somewhat lost among all this cool décor hangs a pastel-hued, child-like, framed birthday card.

This card, carefully crafted by me seventeen years ago, looks like something a six-year-old might have made. Its integrity is saved only by the fact that the main visual element is a gorgeous, cute photo of my smiling youngest baby. Around it I added hand-drawn flowers and hearts and cats and sunshine and butterflies in the softest colours.

Mia turned one in 2001. It was a cause for extra-special celebration, given that she had arrived into the world in a huge hurry, six weeks ahead of schedule and with some serious health issues, which scared us all. In those first days, her future was, well, somewhat uncertain.

In 2001, along with my almost-one-year-old, I had a three-year-old and a teenage daughter of fourteen. I had reduced my working hours from full time to about two-thirds time and I think it would be fair to say that I was finding it all stressful and ridiculously busy.

So a month before Mia's first birthday I handed in my notice, pausing a paid working life that had spanned twenty-two years. I was finally indulging in my dream of an idyllic domestic future. Days in the kitchen in a haze of flour wrapped in a fug of baking as we made buns and chocolate cakes. Autumn walks, even in the rain, afternoons collecting shells on the beach, or in the park feeding the ducks; coming home to light the fire and while away another hour colouring in and drawing. We would be poorer but content. Safe and happy in our domestic bliss.

One of my last big tasks before retiring was to take part in an offsite company presentation. Afterwards I made my way back to the office, feeling relieved and happy that I could now begin the real process of winding down towards my new gentler life. Oh yes, God was in her heaven and all was right with the world.

This was before the days of smartphones and social media, so in my bubble of contentment I casually wandered back into the office and was surprised to find my colleagues gathered around a TV in the boardroom in utter silence. I stared at the screen trying to make sense of what I was seeing. A plane had crashed into the World Trade Centre. It was a beautifully clear, blue sky morning in New York.

'It can't have been an airliner, it must have been a small private jet,' I offered, because an airliner couldn't just crash into the World Trade Centre. And then as we watched live on Sky News, at just after two o'clock, a second plane hit the other tower.

A knot of fear and dread formed in my stomach as the realisation dawned that this was no tragic accident. I stood petrified by the terror that was happening, live on air, in a city that was so familiar. And it just kept getting more horrific. People jumping to their deaths and then the towers collapsing, taking with them the lives of so many more including firefighters and police. The world seemed to be tipping slightly off its axis as these images burned themselves deep into my brain where they live still.

On 14 September Ireland held a national day of mourning. All shops and business were closed. The following day was my baby's first birthday and I had no card.

The world was still engulfed in the news from New York. I tried to shield my youngest two from the replaying horror as it seeped from the radio, TV and newspapers. My dream of an idyllic, gentle, domestic life that I had for so long held in my head and my heart

suddenly seemed to be built on very shaky foundations. Then my three-year-old drew a picture of the towers on fire and I cried at the contamination of innocence.

That great man of peace Gandhi said, 'Be the change you want to see in the world.' And so, in a move reminiscent of the Brits in World War Two and their make-and-do attitude, I raided the three-year-old's crayons and colouring pencils, grabbed a sheet of paper and sat down to illustrate beauty and love in a card for my baby. I am not sure I achieved that. But my amateur effort still serves as a counterpoint to terror and a testament to love and the preservation of innocence.

Orange Over Green

Karl O'Neill

In the late 1960s I wasn't even aware that Armagh had a Gaelic football team. Our neighbours, Down, with three All-Irelands in eight years, rather outshone our lot. And my family was not particularly nationalistic either, despite my great-grandfather being a founding member of the Ulster GAA and, until 1920, hosting many of their committee meetings. Of course, we all played the game in school, but soccer was a greater attraction, and when an inter-community soccer tournament was mooted, about a year after the Troubles started, me and my pals were looking forward to taking part. However, we were called in to a Christian Brother's class and told in no uncertain manner that participation in this soccer tournament would mean we would not be considered for the school's Gaelic football team in the Father Rice Cup. This being 1970, the ban on foreign games was still in place. For some reason, the soccer tournament never materialised.

The first county match I can remember attending was at the local athletic grounds in Armagh a couple of years later. I wasn't terribly interested and turned up some minutes into the game. Someone told me that an Armagh player had already been sent off. His name was Joe Kernan. I hadn't a clue who he was. Some big strapping lout from Crossmaglen. I think the match was against Fermanagh and I can't remember who won. My memory is very hazy about the whole thing.

Armagh had only ever reached one All-Ireland Final. That was in 1953. They lost to Kerry by four points and Bill McCorry missed a penalty. I didn't know who Bill McCorry was but I knew he was the guy who missed the penalty against Kerry. His claim to local infamy.

The fortunes of Armagh's County team were beginning to rise in the mid-1970s, and I began to take a greater interest. Unfortunately, the violence in the North was also on the rise, and by 1976 my parents had decided they'd had enough. By the end of that summer, when I played for my Armagh Harps Under-16 team against Crossmaglen Rangers in the Juvenile County Final in Carrickcruppin – and won – our family had moved south to Dundalk. That was the last Gaelic football match I ever played.

Armagh reached the 1977 Final, and I stood among swathes of orange-flag-waving supporters at the Canal End of Croke Park. As the Armagh team ran out onto the pitch, it was raining. Then the rain stopped, and the Dublin team ran out. It proved somewhat prophetic, as the Dubs gave us a beating, despite that guy Joe Kernan scoring a brace of goals on the day. It had been twenty-four years since Armagh's last Final appearance. It would be twenty-five years to the next.

2002. Third time lucky? The opponents? Kerry. As in 1953.

I sat in the Cusack Stand, and at half-time Armagh, as in '53, were four points behind and had missed a penalty. The ghost of Bill McCorry wafted across the pitch. Some Kerry lads behind me were already offering their condolences. Meanwhile, in the Armagh dressing room, the manager, a certain Joe Kernan, was delivering an iconic half-time talk that spurred on an almighty comeback in the second half and led Oisín McConville, who had missed that earlier penalty, to carry the ghost of Bill McCorry on his classy shoulders and score the only goal of the game. Armagh won by a point.

The orange eruption of emotion that greeted that final whistle was like nothing I have experienced before or since. A mountain of a man beside me kept slapping my back with his hand – I think his fingerprints are still embedded on my spine – as the tears of joy overflowed onto the pitch, orange over green, and the Armagh captain Kieran McGeeney, the Geezer, raised the Holy Grail in the air.

I hesitated to step on to the hallowed ground, feeling somehow unworthy, a fair-weather pilgrim. But I thought of my great-grandfather's devotion in the early days; I thought of Bill McCorry in 1953, his ghost finally laid to rest; I thought of the Christian Brother in 1970 laying down the law; I thought of my final match in Carrickcruppin, and the feel of the trophy in my hands; I thought of the shower of rain in 1977 and our collective yearnings drowned; and I looked at the dancing generations in front of me, 'lost in unthinking joy', and I thought of what these people, my people, had lived through in recent years and how much they deserved this moment.

And I left the stand behind me and walked onto the grass . . .

A Triumph for Freedom in Dublin and South Africa

Liam Power

The fifteen-seater coach approached the Cape Town waterfront under the imposing view of Table Mountain, its flat top covered by spilling cloud to form the iconic 'table cloth'. In the distance, a huddled gathering had assembled, bringing the normal free-flowing traffic to a crawl. A noted celebrity was the magnet. Our driver and guide, Thembo, nonchalantly announced: 'There's a distinguished visitor in town – our president.'

We tourists were flabbergasted to realise we were about to experience a once-in-a-lifetime experience. There on a podium, clearly visible, twenty metres away, stood the iconic and inspirational figure of Nelson Mandela. A sudden surge towards the viewing window of the coach strained necks and brought clicking telescopic cameras to life. It was an ironic coincidence: our planned visit that morning was to District Six Museum, the museum which tells the story of the tyranny that was South Africa's apartheid system. It represented segregation, apartness, humiliation and abuse. White supremacists oppressed fellow humans with a different skin colour. Racism was even enshrined in law.

Just over nine years had elapsed since Mandela's historic inauguration, a relatively short time to undo a culture deeply ingrained. This was all too obvious as later that afternoon we visited one of the many townships that housed millions of those victims. Wooden and tin shacks, in the most primitive and inhumane conditions, is their legacy.

Notwithstanding the poverty of progress, sight cannot be lost for one second of Mandela's heroic and lifelong efforts. He was apartheid's greatest adversary. Following the treason trials he was prepared to die for the cause, but instead was condemned to gaol for twenty-seven harrowing years, eighteen of which were endured on Robben Island.

The next day we visited that unforgiving bastion of incarceration. It was humbling to see where the great Mandela, prisoner number 446/64, had lived. His tiny cell, a 10 x 6ft space, was home to all his possessions: a stray mat for a bed and three thinly worn blankets. With a feeling of guilt I photographed the metal gate and grille of cell number 5.

His outstanding qualities came to light under such barbaric circumstances. Doggedness in campaigning for better conditions and reading materials; discipline in informally teaching fellow prisoners and warders while studying himself; diligence and resourcefulness in how he penned his experiences. Those drafted manuscripts were hidden in flower beds, to eventually become published after his release as his inspirational autobiography, *Long Walk to Freedom*.

Fast forward some months to the evening of the summer solstice of 2003 and his extended walk onto the giant stage, that other field of dreams – Croke Park. The very same Nelson Mandela was the honorary keynote speaker on the occasion of the opening ceremony of the eleventh Special Olympics World Games, the first ever to be held outside of the United States.

A stellar cast of national, sporting and international dignitaries – including our own President Mary McAleese – faded into the background as Mandela, then approaching his eighty-fifth birthday, was helped onto the stage. He spoke of his immense privilege at being present:

Special Olympics is telling testimony of the indestructibility of the human spirit, and of our capacity to overcome hardship and obstacles. You the athletes are ambassadors of the greatness of human kind. You inspire us to know, that all obstacles to human

achievement and progress are surmountable. Your achievements remind us of the potential to greatness that resides in all of us.

What profound words coming from the man who not only talked the talk, but truly walked the walk. I felt that his presence and the values he represented had significant parallels with the concept of disabilities and the Special Olympic movement. These special athletes were reaching out as individuals, to highlight and demonstrate their own freedom, to showcase their ability.

This statesman promoted the cause of the underprivileged like no other global messenger before or since. In tandem with the games' motto, 'Let me win, but if I can't win, let me be brave in the attempt', his appearance not only brought history to life, but also shook hands with the flame of hope.

An Exile in Liverpool

Kevin Barry

In the early winter of 2004, feeling a bit low, in that Novemberish way, I decided to take up birdwatching. I thought that it would get me out of the house, at least, and keep me away from the mope of my thoughts. The notion of fresh air is always close to the Irish neurotic's heart. A dose of fresh air and a few strong cups of tea would get you through an apocalypse, or so we convince ourselves . . .

So I went down to the nearest camera and binoculars shop. I was living, at this time, in the old financial district of Liverpool, on the streets near the Albert Dock that once made up the world capital of shipping insurance. I had a long, vivid discussion with the elderly man who ran the shop there. As we stood outside his store and tried out a few pairs, training them on the gigantic stone Liver Birds that perch famously on the clock tower of the Royal Liver Building down at Pier Head, he told me what the view had looked like in the early 1960s . . .

You could almost walk across the Mersey to Birkenhead, he said, so dense was the boat traffic on the river then, and he remembered it as a time of great excitement for the city, a time of immensity, with the city at last throwing off the austerity of the post-war era and opening itself to a new age, new ideas, and, of course, new music.

By 2004 it was a melancholy scene – the river was mostly empty, the loading docks having moved down the estuary and out of town. The famous Albert Dock was left a ghostly, heritage-era relic of itself, and there was just the mournful back and forth of the ferry across the Mersey . . .

There is always at least one job available in Liverpool, by the way, and it's on the Birkenhead ferry, because they play the Gerry and the Pacemakers song on a loop, all day every day – '*Feeerry cross the Meeeersey*' – and employees tend to last about three weeks before they run screaming to the job centre.

But anyway I bought the binoculars and I became a twitcher that winter – I was out morning until night, going down to Delamere Forest to see the lapwings over the lake and the kestrels hover above the cold, wintry woods as the light thickened; I was going out to the Formby shore to see the migrant geese, and the little oyster-catchers as they busily dug out a living on the tideline.

It worked ... I cheered up ... Watching the birds somehow brought me back within the realm of myself ... Or it may be more accurate to say that it usefully distracted me from myself ... I started to write my stories again.

I was in romantic exile from the country where my stories occurred but it was a close exile – on a clear night, you could almost shout across the Irish Sea and the cousins would hear you. But it was an exile just about far enough to put the place in perspective, to explain to me, as the sentences emerged, what it was I loved about Ireland, and what I hated, and I could feel that the stories were starting to work out for me on the page.

Liverpool was being dug up. They were building an enormous new shopping district. It felt as if it was in transition from one kind of city to another, but the process seemed uncertain, tentative, the future sketchy and vague – it's the kind of transition a writer can understand. We are always feeling our way in the dark.

As winter deepened, I wandered the streets quite happily – it was a lovely thing to see Strawberry Fields and Penny Lane flagged up on the buses. It was lovely, too, to be able to name the birds of the city, from the most ragged little sparrows hopping the bins on Bold Street to the majestic peregrine falcons who had begun to nest in abandoned warehouses on the docks.

The city was friendly to the point of homicide – it clutched you so closely to its bosom it could squeeze all the life out of you.

Its old gin palace pubs warmed the spirit on a winter's night; the bracing walks by the chill, grey river opened up the mind to a kind of dreaming.

I think of it still as a literary city and of my brief few years there as a critical part of my apprenticeship. If I was never precisely happy at the time in Liverpool, I was happy at least in retrospect. As soon I left the place I loved it, and I pined for it awfully.

Doings in Japan

Caitriona Lally

In 2005 my boyfriend and I went to Japan to teach English. We lived in a small city in the north, which merited half a page in the *Lonely Planet* guide: 'A rather unsightly port city, Kushiro fails to captivate tourists.' Kushiro, we were repeatedly told, had the third-best sunset in the world. A neighbouring city was noted for having the second-longest park bench in the world. One of Kushiro's top ten sightseeing highlights was its roundabout.

Given such underwhelming endorsements, very few foreigners lived in the city, so we were treated as minor celebrities. In supermarkets we posed for photos with children and signed autographs. Once, I got to the till to find a line of small children trailing behind me, Pied Piper-style. Worse, when we went to hot spring baths, young girls would follow me from bath to bath, giggling and pointing at my naked body.

In schools, children would hang off me, poking at my eyes and measuring their hand against mine, horrified at its size. It got awkward when some of the smaller children cried when I walked into the classroom. I was often the first Western person they'd seen and, as one teacher helpfully pointed out, I had 'the big legs'. Older children would gasp and roar '*Dekai!*' when I entered a classroom. I later asked my boss what it meant. He said: 'Large, very large, used to describe an enormous mammal like an elephant or whale.' I didn't tell him why I'd asked.

When I taught children, I showed pictures to introduce them to Ireland: Kylemore Abbey, Irish wolfhounds, Roy Keane. But with my limited Japanese providing no context, the children came away thinking all Irish people lived in castles, played professional football and owned gigantic dogs that ate the marauding wolves.

In teaching adults about Ireland, I might have placed too much emphasis on the Famine or maybe I didn't clarify that this was a historical event, because the following week I was inundated with presents of cakes and fruit and dried fish with eyeballs still intact.

We experienced many small earthquakes or tremors that year, but one afternoon, I was teaching a class of ten-year-olds when an earthquake measuring over 5 on the Richter scale struck. The room jolted like an aeroplane hitting turbulence; doors and windows rattled, and in one sudden move, the children dived under their desks, closely followed by me. Seeing the surprise on the students' faces, I realised the class teacher's legs were still in a vertical position. I sheepishly crept out, pretending I was checking on the children, and then stood up as if I'd never been anywhere but standing. When the shaking stopped, the principal made a PA announcement about a tsunami. The children cheered and returned to their seats, but I didn't have enough Japanese to understand anything beyond the word 'tsunami'. After some furious miming of tidal waves left me none the wiser, I drew a large wave on the blackboard followed by a question mark, and finally got a reassuring 'No' from the teacher.

Learning Japanese with its three alphabets was challenging. There were no street names or signs, so I bumbled around a new language and a new city in a continual fog of confusion. Entire supermarket shelves were a mystery, full of products I wasn't familiar with, labelled in alphabets I couldn't read.

Snow made the city even more difficult to navigate. Kushiro is one of Japan's coldest cities, covered in several feet of snow for five months of the year, hitting the minus 20s some nights. We put tinfoil on the windows of the apartment to keep in the heat. On the coldest days, if you filled a glass of water in the morning, a crust of ice would have formed by evening. It was a topsy-turvy world where you put things *into* the fridge to keep them warm.

Japanese politeness was difficult to grasp. Blowing your nose in public is frowned upon, so having a cold meant performing all kinds of contortions with a tissue for the sake of discretion. Greetings were also an issue. When I was introduced to the mother of a student, I shook her hand with what I thought was enthusiasm, but my boss later told me this level of vigour would be considered an act of violence in Japan. Bowing was even more fraught, however: companies sent their employees on bowing courses to learn the precise angle depending on difference in age or rank, but I never mastered it and was in permanent fear of toppling onto the person I was bowing to, or worse, headbutting them.

Coming back to Ireland was a culture shock: we had to get used to our loss of celebrity again, but at least greeting people here couldn't result in life-changing injury.

Why I Started to Write

Melatu Uche Okorie

In 2006 three very significant things happened to me: I came to Ireland. I became a mother. I started to write. I wrote because there were many occurrences around me that I wanted to keep in my memory.

Some were stories of sadness, grief and betrayal. Some were stories of survival and freedom. Sometimes these stories would come to me. This would be when a friend would say after they had had a bad day: 'Go and bring a pen and paper, and I will tell you my story. It will fill many pages, I promise you!'

Sometimes I found the stories, because a direct provision accommodation centre in 2006 was like a small UN convention centre. One quickly learned about everyone else: if they had parents who were still living; if they had children they had left behind in their countries; or how they found Ireland upon arrival; and if the person was a loner and did not like the company of others, the story of the person would be pieced together by some watchful eyes.

There were also occasions for certain kind of talk. Conversations about surviving families – those who had passed and how they passed – might take place at a gathering to celebrate the birth of a new baby, while a get-together to rejoice over the granting of a refugee status might prompt reflections on people's first few days in Ireland.

According to Dee, her arrival in Ireland was marred by experiences surrounding the birth of her child. She started her story by reminding us of how the birth of a child should be the best time for a family and how it was only recently that she started to celebrate the birth of her child:

'I went into labour upon arrival at the reception centre. I wasn't even in pain. I just started vomiting and stooling. I did not realise it was a sign of being in labour. I had no one to ask, no parents, no siblings. No past to draw on. When there was no relief from my diahorrea, the people at the reception centre office called an ambulance for me. As soon as I arrived at the hospital, I was rushed to the delivery room because the baby was on its way out.

'Everything happened so quickly, which was good. But it was afterwards . . . when there was no one to call to share the news of my delivery. The local woman in my ward had people coming in and out to visit her, bringing her gifts and balloons. When it was time to leave the hospital, I was given a voucher for a bus. I carried my baby out and stood at the bus stop, a woman alone, inconspicuous to the people around me. I don't think anyone even noticed the tears running down my face.'

The year 2006 was filled with tales like Dee's. As women and children migrated into Ireland, stories like these were commonplace around the hostels. But Dee's story stood out among our group of friends. She had a way of silencing us when we tried to tell our stories, for she would point out the little things we had that we had taken for granted. She would remind us of things such as: 'Your husband was there with you when that happened, was he not?' 'You have parents and siblings who are still living, do you not?' Or, 'you have people from your country who came out to help you when that happened, did you not?'

But even someone like Dee can only lament the loss of one eye until she meets a person with no eyes, and that was exactly what happened one evening at a get-together in a resident's room. We were joined by a new face, Yee, who had just been moved to our accommodation centre with her two children.

When our conversation that evening shifted to the loneliness of being in a new country, Dee shared the story of when she went to the hospital to give birth again. We would have quickly moved to a less emotive topic after that if Yee had not spoken up. Her voice was low, and she spoke with a slow assurance that made us listen attentively.

'The day I arrived in Ireland,' she said, 'I was in the room they gave me feeding my oldest son. He was eleven months old at the time and I was twenty-six weeks pregnant with my younger son when I felt a sharp pain. The pain increased rapidly until I could not continue feeding my son or even sit up straight. I managed to lie down on my bed. My things were littered all over the floor because I was still unpacking. I think I was even about to lose consciousness when an African woman walked in. I did not know she was sharing the room with me at the time. She must have been the one who got help for me.

'When the ambulance arrived, the paramedics said they were going to take me to the hospital. The girl who registered me at the reception centre asked if I had anyone who could take care of my son. I shook my head, no. The paramedics said that I would not be able to go with my son, that I would have to leave him behind. As they were wheeling me out, my son holding on to the hand of the girl from the reception centre, I saw the African woman who had entered the room earlier. Our eyes met, and I said to her, "Please, can you help me to hold my son while I go to the hospital?" She said, "Yes sister, no problem." You know, over there, things are very different from the way it is here. In that hostel, everybody used to be afraid and would not even talk to each other.

'I ended up staying at the hospital for six days. They did not even want to discharge me, but for the fact that I was crying so much that I wanted to go home. Oh, when I saw my son again . . .' Yee sighed and shook her head before suddenly letting out a soft laugh. 'The woman I left him with was calling him Ben because I did not even tell her my son's name before I left for the hospital that day!'

The next time I saw Dee after the evening with Yee, she beckoned to me.

'Did you hear that woman's story?' she asked as soon as I got to a suitable talking distance.

'My God, I know!' I replied, shaking my head in wonder.

Her next question made me stop. 'How can one even compete with that?'

Topsoil

Siobhán Mannion

2007. NASA launches its *Dawn* space mission, to explore the two largest bodies in the main asteroid belt.

Here on Earth, the year begins with a big move into a new home, boxing up and unpacking our lives inside not-yet-familiar rooms.

Bringing to mind the houses in which, decades earlier, my parents had established themselves.

A nurse and an engineer from the West of Ireland, making their way in England.

Our first tiny abode had doubled as my father's workplace, from where he made calls about drawings and measurements, digger drivers, machine hire, quantities of cement and topsoil.

Later, four offspring in tow, there was the second house, with more space to circulate amidst its constant clatter of activity and clamour of voices . . .

. . . before the gradual subtraction around the kitchen table, including the early loss of our mother.

From 2007 onwards, as *Dawn* continued on its voyage, to study the diverse characteristics of its two destinations, Vesta and Ceres . . .

. . . we, a father and four now-adult children, moved through another ten years.

My siblings had families of their own. All of us floating regularly in and out of each other's day-to-day worlds.

Until the shock of an emergency surgery, signalling the grip of serious illness, and we gathered, orbiting the remaining parent, untethered from daily routine.

On his return to the house, he begins by walking around the garden, tentatively, newly aware of the body's limitations. Setting targets of two laps . . . then three . . . and four.

Soon after, he undertakes to make it around the block. Each of us, along with his partner, taking turns to accompany him.

Always active, not quite fully retired, he trains his attention now on the incremental changes in the season; enjoys the cherry blossoms, wonders how long they will remain arched over the road in full bloom.

Other unspoken thoughts, as we marched together, detached from the rhythms of ordinary working days. On one occasion pausing to listen as two women played cello in a front room.

Above us, *Dawn* had by now become the first-ever spacecraft to successfully go into orbit around two different destinations, travelling first to Vesta – the surface of which it discovers to be rocky and dry – and later to Ceres, which is icy.

Scientists chart how the place where each one was formed affected how it evolved.

During the first six months post-op, there is a potential recovery in the making.

Life in the ascendant. Not without its considerable challenges but punctuated by laughter, more people than ever crammed around the kitchen table, a trip back to Ireland. Until the finding, scanned and visible, that at a cellular level, my father's body has ultimately conspired against him.

Not long afterwards, this person of energy and action is struggling on our short walks, seeking respite on the previously unremarkable structure of a nearby low garden wall.

I recall my mother, twenty-five years earlier, standing at their bedroom window, looking out at the trees: 'I won't be here to see them change colour,' she said.

We lost him during the quiet of a heavy snow, the blizzard delaying his final journey home.

A few months later I am alone in my father's house and read that the *Dawn* spacecraft has run out of hydrazine fuel. After its historic eleven-year mission, NASA announces on 1 November 2018 that it has become a so-called 'celestial monument', and will never again communicate with Earth.

My focus is on material things.

Shirts on hangers: washed, pressed, ready to be given away. Stacks of books and photographs. Unopened current affairs magazines. Souvenir mugs from different continents. In his office, piles of paper folders relating to road-building contracts.

The accumulations of a life; all the doing done.

I am here, dismantling spaces, clearing away the personal, to allow strangers to map their future onto these rooms.

I take a break, walk the familiar loop, breathing in the chilly air of late afternoon. The trees, so recently ablaze in autumnal pink-gold, now almost bare.

My life is here, and elsewhere.

Just beyond halfway, at the end of the neighbouring road, I cut the corner, at the point where we would both veer off the pavement – in tandem, in conversation – and step onto the soil.

Already, this day is falling away. The oncoming twilight freighted with our distant pasts and unlived futures.

Dirt clings to my shoes, leaving tiny traces, as I track our old route in the descending winter light.

V
2008–2017

Setting the Scene

Lisa McInerney

It's very often on my travels I'm told that we're experiencing *a golden age of Irish writing* and asked, then, why that is? The answer is obvious to me. Writers seek to document, to understand what's going on in their communities and to translate that into prose, or poetry, or drama. To reflect on what it means to be a particular person in a particular society and tell that story, to find the truth in it, the beauty in it, the madness in it. Even the most determined practitioner of auto-fiction knows none of us exists without the rest. And so, when Ireland is at her most troublesome, the Irish writers are at their most alert. Who can resist the urge to document their country when their country keeps redefining herself?

In 2008, after a few years of our thinking we were very sophis-ticated altogether – a few years of notions and hot air – the Celtic Tiger deflated, lay down in a ditch, and let the weeds grow over him. That property bubble popped and we were left with a film covering the country, the fatty skin of a bad idea. It was desperate. We were desperate, not least because we were forced to redefine ourselves again. We had been poor cousins to the rest of Europe for so long, up there in the North Atlantic with our mouths gaping, and now it seemed we'd failed to fledge, that despite all those years training for it, psyching ourselves up, we were on the ground under the eave with both wings broken. So much for the SSIAs and the rental properties on the continent.

A number of my colleagues have pointed out that the dole was fertiliser for this golden age of Irish writing, that if the country hadn't experienced that economic crash we'd all be working as mortgage advisers for online banks, that the combination of free time to write with a feeling of there being nothing left to lose inspired a generation not just to make art, but to take risks with form and content. I think, too, it was a sense of alienation from the idea of Ireland, we'd been fed in the previous decade, which provoked a desire to challenge notions about Irishness. Not being able to get a grip on who we were triggered a mad desire to get a grip on who we were.

I started this past decade writing short, sarcastic pieces online about the state of the place. I did so because the SSIA and continental-rental property picture seemed so cartoonish, a kind of cover version of Bel Air created by spoofers and chancers, full of socialites and celebrity solicitors (I'm still not sure how we managed that). I tried to make these short pieces funny, but the humour was spiked with fury: I was angry, as a lot of working-class people were angry, about how we were excluded from this glossy national image, about how our reality was deemed unnecessary when composing the country's character and assessing her needs. These short pieces struck a chord. A shared sense of unease, a bone to pick with the country.

I was working in Cork when the roof caved in. For years I looked after the front desk for a construction company. When I started there, the place buzzed with Irish and Polish accents. By the time I left, the factory was manned only sparsely, and a number of the offices had been closed to save on heat and electricity, the remaining staff members clustered on the ground floor. We went through a number of rounds of redundancies and pay cuts. Don't worry, my boss told me. I promise we won't cut your pay. This was not a noble declaration: I was on the minimum wage. A general election was called in 2011, just when things seemed at their worst. Turnout was low among my friends. We were most of us young parents, too broke to emigrate, and too sure of what was coming to try to head it off. Even seven years ago it was a different Ireland, characterised by resignation. Even the anger felt beige.

But we've been busy. In the past three years alone we've fought for and won marriage equality and reproductive rights, in a country we were once sure was far too Catholic to entertain either. We've watched the rise of the far right from our left-leaning enclave, considered it as an ugly response to desperate migration, seen European integrity threatened by the reckless chauvinism of the crowd next door, been asked to think again about the possibility of a United Ireland. We've gawped across the Atlantic in horror. We've flatly refused to pay water charges. We've woken the feminists. We've marched in response to an appalling housing crisis. The only constant we have is Michael D. Higgins and Michael D. Higgins is a passionate advocate for progression; in 2018 you can hardly get a handle on the status quo.

Imagine the writing we're going to get out of that.

The Start of a
New Life in Ireland

Bernadett Buda

If anyone asked me how I knew ten years ago that Ireland was where I wanted to live, I would simply say: I didn't. As with most stories of emigration, local connections, goodwill and a bit of luck all played their part. I didn't know much about the Emerald Isle, apart from its breathtaking scenery, mild climate and friendly people. And that they spoke English – a language which, in my naivety, I *thought* I had a good command of.

I arrived in January 2008. Despite the rain that hit me straight in the face as soon as I stepped off the plane, I had a bright outlook on my future in a new country. If the Celtic Tiger had been showing signs of failing health, no one seemed to know or care. Within two weeks, I landed a decent job and did my best to settle in as quickly as I could.

Straight away I noticed there was a distinct air of generosity around, so different from what I had been used to in Hungary. When I went to the post office to pay the gas bill, the clerk behind the counter asked me as if it were a matter of course: 'Would you like to pay the whole lot now?' Coming from Eastern Europe, I was completely taken aback. Is there any choice? Does he mean I can actually pay as much of the bill I want now, and then come back later with the balance if and when I feel like it? Just as I would have at home, I paid in full, but I couldn't help thinking: what a country!

Another sign of abundance was the number of babies being pushed around in buggies, those same buggies laden with shopping bags full of new clothes. The demographics of Ireland were clearly in a healthy state and people had enough disposable income to go on a shopping spree on a weekly basis. I too, soon joined the masses – I mean, on the shopping sprees. As far as rearing the future generation is concerned, I have to admit I didn't make any contribution.

Sadly, in the autumn of 2008 it became clear that the Celtic Tiger had actually been about to draw his last breath just as I was stepping off the plane back in January – don't look at me, I had nothing to do with it! Ireland faced into some very difficult times, as practically the whole world spiralled into an economic downturn that year. And yet my own memories of that time are happy, as I continued to settle in. Forget the economy! More importantly, What shall I wear tomorrow? was my take on Irish life. I found it a real challenge to make smart clothing choices in the Irish weather.

I must have been here for about two months when I innocently asked a colleague at work: 'When is it going to stop raining?' She looked at me as if contemplating whether I was in my right mind and replied: 'Never?'

The weather forecast was hardly a help. On a bad day they'd say: 'Showers with sunny spells.' On a good day the report would change to: 'Sunny spells with showers.' I learned to dress like an onion and carry around half of my wardrobe, including spare shoes and a rain-coat, to counteract the sometimes horizontal Irish rain. Right from the early days I could tell Irish and non-Irish apart just by what they were wearing. On a sunny day, ladies in tights? Definitely not Irish. Fifteen degrees and a bit of sunshine always brought out bare, snow-white Irish legs and arms. Thankfully, the body adjusts with time. One has to be patient. If I remember correctly, my toes eventually saw the Irish sun. In 2010.

Another vital part of my adjustment process was getting the hang of the Irish accent and turns of phrase. If I liked some colloquialism I heard, I incorporated it into my chat. That's why I soon proudly began to open conversations with 'How's the farm?' When I first heard it, I thought, isn't this a lovely phrase? It seems to hail from olden days when most people had their own farms in the country-side. Surely it has been around for generations and has even wound its way into the vernacular of urban dwellers. It made perfect sense.

The Irish, bless them, didn't bat an eyelid. Never mind anyone ever enlightening me that it's not the farm, for heaven's sake, but the 'form'! Oh well, at least I tried . . .

I soon realised that many Irish are capable of spicing up the English language, breaking and making rules in the process. Was it a coincidence that Sebastian Barry's novel *The Secret Scripture* was published in 2008? You cannot often say about a book that its sentences touch the deepest chords in your heart, even though they are describing scenes and notions that are alien to you. This book did just that. It deepened my understanding of my adopted country, and gave me an appreciation for Irish literary talent. I went on to discover Roddy Doyle, Frank McCourt, John Banville and Edna O'Brien, and from there, some of the new writers now making waves on the literary scene.

So, in my first ten years here – a lot of reading. A lot of talking. And a lot of getting rained on.

I can think of worse ways to get to know and love a country.

Switch

Danielle McLaughlin

It's June 2009 and I'm at home in Cork standing at the foot of our stairs. I'm feeling strange, fluey; I should go to bed, I think, sleep it off. I wake the next morning to find that my fingers and toes have begun to curl in on themselves, claw-like. Over the coming days, my movements become more restricted until simple things I've always taken for granted, like dressing, and using the bathroom, become slow and painful. As my joints grow swollen and puffy, bones press white and tight against my skin as if trying to break free. They are rising up, engaging in an act of mutiny. They are revolting.

The world, Thackeray said, gives back to every man a reflection of his own face. While I was being dragged under by this mysterious illness, Ireland, and the world, was in the grip of swine flu. Illness, in the world of literature, has shaped many a narrative arc, and has often been credited with a blooming of artistic ability. The tragic death of the beautiful consumptive is the trope of many a Victorian novel. Is it wrong of me to wish that my country had delivered a more romantic metaphor than a respiratory disease of pigs? Swine flu does not conjure up visions of Keats, Shelley, Katherine Mansfield, Charlotte Brontë. It is not a romantic disease. But then neither was the confounding illness that soon left me unable to work.

2009, at the age of forty, was the year I came to understand the meaning of the word *can't*.

Before that, I was a solicitor with my own practice, which I'd upgraded from a home office to a new city-centre premises. Within weeks of becoming ill, I'd transferred all my clients to another firm. It was a seismic shift. Becoming a lawyer was something on which I'd fixed my sights as a teenager. To realise the dream, I'd spent many years attending college as an evening student. Almost overnight it was gone, the speed with which it came to an end inversely proportional to the length of time it had taken to achieve.

Swine flu, for its part, also moved quickly: just six weeks between identification of the first cases in Mexico and the declaration of a global pandemic.

My illness stopped me in my tracks, psychologically as well as physically. I wasn't used to being stopped. *Can't* was a word for other people. I hadn't countenanced it before. I came of age in an era when the popular refrain was 'You can do it.' 'You can do anything.' I'd listened to my kids, as pre-schoolers, sing along to Bob the Builder: *Can we fix it? Yes we can!* Well, it turned out that, actually, I couldn't. I was simply too sick. I had to stop. *Can't.* It was a revelation.

2009 also brought revelations of a darker kind. The Ryan and Murphy reports make for heartbreaking reading, detailing as they do abuses of power perpetrated on the most vulnerable. The Murphy Report found there was little or no concern for the welfare of abused children. Complainants were often met with denial, arrogance and cover-up. It's sobering to imagine how many lives might not have been ruined had Ireland swung into action against child abuse the way it did against swine flu, if child abuse, too, had been treated as an emergency.

I shall spare you a litany of my medical complaints. Mine is not a sad story. It was in time discovered that I'd experienced a rare reaction to a medication, which had affected my liver function and triggered a longer-term chronic condition, a form of autoimmune arthritis.

While I was very ill, and no longer practising law, I had a sense that something had broken in me. I'd found law to be an immensely creative career; I loved the focus on words. And then there was the drama, the stories, the courtroom performances in

all the glorious specifics of their evidence. No longer having any clients to advise, I began to write and soon got sucked down the rabbit hole of fiction. I never returned to legal practice. Looking back on that time, I don't regard my career as having been ended by illness. Rather, like a locomotive, it was shunted onto a different set of tracks. I'm still someone who makes her living by interrogating words and stories, just in a different way.

Meanwhile, swine flu has been vanquished, a vaccine developed. Consumption, on the other hand, or tuberculosis as it is latterly known, claims more lives today than it did in the nineteenth century; 98 per cent of these deaths occur in the developing world. It seems that it is not considered an emergency.

Extramural

Janet Moran

2010 was, mostly, not great for me. Being an unemployed actor can feel like a particularly useless thing to be and by September of that year, I was broke, alone and living in a cold, small flat with little to do. I've always been interested in history and, in fact, immersing myself in history books about particular periods has often been the thing that has got me through hard times before. I forget how, but I learned that one could study humanities in Trinity as an extramural student. This meant that while I did not have to hand up essays or take exams, I could attend lectures twice a week. It would give me a reason to get up on those days and perhaps feel not quite as bootless as I had been feeling. It could become my job. I decided to take the course called 'Europe after 1870'.

With first day of school nerves and a new notebook in hand, I sidled through the arts block, bluffing the air of a constituent. Sitting at the back of the lecture hall, I could see a lot of computer screens open on Facebook, screens that didn't necessarily change once the lecture began. Just like in American movies, we seemed to have segregated ourselves from the start. The middle section was made up of the just-left schoolers, the front rows seemed to be made up of mature students – or 'Noddies' as they were known due to their enthusiasm. And the back rows contained us, the extramuralers. We were exclusively made up of what seemed to be retired women, unemployed me, and Joe.

Right from the first lecture, I wanted to be his friend. He was charismatic, with a kind face and a Slovakian accent unsullied by many years in his adopted home. For the second lecture, I manoeuvred myself into the seat beside him and afterwards we had a good chat about what we'd just learned. After the third, we decided to go for coffee. He told me that he had come because his daughter had bought him the course as a gift following the death of his wife. I told him about me not having much purpose at the time and feeling a bit lost.

He said 'I will bring you luck. I bring people luck.'

'Really?'

'Naturally.'

And so, twice-weekly coffees became twice-weekly lunches. And history lectures became history lunches. Obscure little pearls of knowledge became mine. Like the fact that Goebbels had been a champagne salesman in France before the war. Or that while fighting against the Nazis in Ukraine, a Moscow symphony orchestra had come to play for Joe's regiment, and become trapped and so stayed and played every night for them for weeks, in the forest. First-hand experience of the Austro-Hungarian Empire. Details of dancing lessons in Slovakia in the twenties. An escape from Prague following an international table-tennis incident, involving Tito. Life as a refugee in Switzerland. The chance meeting with a man who owned a garage in Dublin that led Joe and his family to seek refuge in Cabra instead of Australia. Australia's loss. Coaching the Irish table-tennis team. Translating for Jack Charlton in Europe.

'Really?'

'Naturally.'

All these lives and I was barely managing to fill one.

But now I had my guide through the twentieth century.

The lunches became trips to Glencree to pick blueberries, events at the Slovakian Embassy, plays at the Dublin Theatre Festival where once Joe mistook an immersive piece and began berating an actor who he felt was being rude to another actor. Never a bystander.

Walking from Trinity to YO! Sushi each time for our lunch was like hanging out with a rock star. We'd be stopped every few feet by someone who loved him and wanted to share a few quick words. The waiters and waitresses in every café we went to who would sit with us. The homeless people he never passed. You see, people genuinely light up around him. The vivacity and vividness with which he lives his life is infectious. The undimmed curiosity and vitality.

When the course came to an end the following spring, Joe gave the final lecture, as the second term had covered 1918 to the present day. The span of his life. We decided to study The Enlightenment the following year, the Industrial Revolution another year, but then as I got busier with work and as I met my partner and had my son, I skived off from our studies. But I'd learned an abundance. How to be grateful, how to persevere, how to live. And sitting at his hundredth birthday party recently, among his family and an eclectic bunch of friends, it landed on me again.

'You know, you really did bring me luck.'

'Naturally.'

Oh Wow!

Mary Morrissy

He was a hippie, a computer nerd, a tech guru. He launched products he'd designed on giant stages to crowded auditoriums wearing his trademark black polo necks and blue jeans, with the zeal of a religious preacher. He revolutionised how we use and look at technology.

'Design is not just what it looks like and feels like,' he said, 'design is how it works.'

Steve Jobs was a co-founder of Apple Inc. and in time he became synonymous with the sleek technology he designed. He was, by all accounts, a difficult man – often described as a bully – who had stormy and combative relationships with those close to him, particularly with his eldest daughter, Lisa, who was born, when he was twenty-three, on a hippie commune in Oregon. For many years he refused to acknowledge that Lisa was his daughter while her mother struggled to raise her alone on welfare.

In her memoir, *Small Fry*, Lisa remembers that in 1980, when Jobs was sued for paternity, he swore in a deposition that he was sterile and named another man as her father. Yet when he designed his first mass-market computer – a forerunner to the Macintosh – he called it Lisa. The court ordered Jobs to pay support payments of $385 per month. Four days later Apple went public and he was worth more than $200 million, but the maintenance payments remained the same.

But Jobs' own family story was a tangled web, stranger than any fiction, which became, literally, the stuff of fiction.

Jobs' biological father was 'John' Jandali, a Syrian Muslim from Homs, who met his mother, Joanne Schieble, when they were both students at the University of Wisconsin in the early 1950s. Joanne's father was against the relationship but in 1954 she fell pregnant, and because of family opposition, she decided to give the baby up for adoption. Six weeks later, Joanne's father died and the couple decided to marry. They had a daughter, Mona, two years later, but the couple divorced in 1962 and Jandali returned to Syria. Joanne remarried and Mona took her stepfather's name, becoming Mona Simpson.

Remember that name.

In 1986 Steve Jobs set about finding his natural mother and when he did, he discovered he had a sister whom he knew nothing about. The same was true of Mona – she had never been told she had a brother put up for adoption. 'Mona was not completely thrilled at first to have me in her life, and have her mother so emotionally affectionate toward me,' Jobs told his biographer, but as they got to know one another the siblings became very close. 'She is my family. I don't know what I'd do without her.'

Together Steve and Mona set about trying to track down their father, who had by the 1980s returned to the US. But when they found him, Steve decreed that only Mona would meet him in person. Jandali had moved into the restaurant business and when they met, he told Mona he had once managed a Mediterranean restaurant in San Jose. All of the successful technology people used to patronise the place, he boasted to Mona, even Steve Jobs! When Mona told Steve this, he recalled meeting Jandali. 'He was Syrian,' Jobs recalled, 'balding. We shook hands.'

But he refused to meet Jandali as his father. 'I was a wealthy man by then, and I didn't trust him not to try to blackmail me or go to the press about it . . .' he said.

Mona Simpson is an award-winning writer, who, even before she met Steve Jobs, had also searched for her family but through her fiction. Her first novel, *Anywhere but Here*, about struggling single mother Adele and her teenage daughter Ann, was adapted into a film of the same name starring Susan Sarandon and Natalie Portman. A sequel, *The Lost Father*, features Ann going to the Middle East in search of the Egyptian father who has abandoned her. Her third novel, *A Regular Guy*, from the mid-1990s – after she and Jobs had discovered one another – explores the strained relationship of a Silicon Valley tycoon with his daughter born out of wedlock.

The novel created strain between Mona and Steve's daughter Lisa, who felt Simpson had traduced their relationship to write the book. Similarly, Mona Simpson decried Lisa's memoir, *Small Fry*, which, she said, differed dramatically from her memories of him.

But when Jobs was diagnosed with pancreatic cancer in 2003, these family rifts were temporarily set aside. The extended family, including Jobs' wife and three other children, kept vigil as his health visibly declined. Mona was by his bedside when he died on 5 October 2011. It was she who delivered the eulogy at his memorial service, describing their meeting in their twenties.

'Even as a feminist,' she said, 'my whole life I'd been waiting for a man to love, who could love me. For decades, I'd thought the man would be my father. When I was twenty-five, I met that man and he was my brother.'

His final words, she told the congregation, were, 'Oh wow, oh wow, oh wow.'

And if that name Mona Simpson rings a bell then yes, you've guessed it: Mona Simpson is the name of Homer Simpson's mother in *The Simpsons*. The real Mona Simpson's husband, Richard Appel – yes, Appel – was a screenwriter on the series and named Bart's zany political activist grandmother after his wife.

Meeting The Boss

Robert Higgins

When I was young, my father and I had what could politely be described as musical differences. While I was mostly interested in the gangster rap that was dominating the airwaves in the mid-2000s, he was intent on introducing me to the sort of music that had shaped him as a young man. The likes of Leonard Cohen, Van Morrison and Paul Simon were always on heavy rotation on his stereo, but there was one artist who stood out above all the rest.

To say that my dad was a big Bruce Springsteen fan would be an understatement. He had based significant portions of his personality on him and listening to him describe his youth of racing in the street and hanging out on the boardwalk one would wonder whether the line between Bruce's songs and his own life had been permanently blurred. We did live in Longford after all.

He often said he was the one singer whose hand he would like to shake and he spoke about how he would like to meet him.

It was 2012 by the time he decided it was time for me and my younger brother to experience Springsteen in the live arena. Bruce was playing in the RDS and we made the pilgrimage up from Longford that evening. Despite me and my brother's initial scepticism, we were blown away. Bruce performed like a man possessed. For more than three hours, he entertained the crowd using every trick in the book. By the encore, myself and my brother were tired, spent and converted.

After the gig ended and the band had left the stage, we filed out among the throngs of people. Myself and my brother were heading towards the car when our father stopped us. 'We're not going home yet.' As we walked, he explained his plan. Earlier in the week, he had received a tip-off that Bruce would be staying at a local hotel. Our dad wasn't the sort of man who was ever too bothered with fame, but if his all-time favourite musician was drinking down the road, there was no way he was missing out on a potential sing-song.

We arrived outside the plush hotel, none of us feeling particularly confident about gaining access. The doorman gave myself and my brother a hard stare as we approached but when they saw us flanked by our elderly companion, he stepped aside and allowed us entry to the bar without requesting proof of residence.

We installed ourselves at the bar and waited with bated breath. After about an hour of feeling out of place we were beginning to lose hope. We were about to call it a night when suddenly the door opened and in walked Bruce's right-hand man, Silvio Dante himself, Stevie Van Zandt, decked out in his signature bandana and followed by the rest of the E Street Band. It looked like it was happening after all. We kept an eye on the door, awaiting the main man's entrance. We sat there for another hour, one eye on the door, one eye on the clock. It was getting late and our hopes were once again lagging when there was a rumble in the hall. We froze, wondering if this was the moment, whether Bruce was finally going to reveal himself. The door creaked open, people held their breath, bartenders stopped serving and in walked . . . Bono.

A look of disbelief spread across my father's face.

Bono strutted into the party, ordered a bottle of red wine, installed himself in the middle of the E Street Band and quickly became master of ceremonies.

'I don't believe it,' my father said, shaking his head. The night went on with Bono now the life and soul of the party. Bruce never showed and we decided it was time to leave sometime around one. We tried to console our father with the old platitude about it being better to never meet your heroes.

The evening was not fruitless however. Since that night, myself and my brother have become just as big fans as our father and have seen Bruce Springsteen on each subsequent visit to Ireland.

Every so often, when I'm home for the weekend, my dad will call me in to the room, put on an old vinyl from one of the records and we'll chat about the night that we almost met The Boss.

A Call for Help

Emilie Pine

In February 2013 I telephoned a woman I had never met.

'Hi Pavla,' I said when she answered. 'You don't know me. I'm Richard's daughter. I'm sorry to phone so early on a Sunday, but I think my dad is dying.'

Pavla was my dad's closest friend on the Greek island where he'd made his home since 2001. He had moved there from Ireland, she was from Prague, being from elsewhere and falling in love with Corfu was what they had in common. She was the only person I knew I could call who would not let him down.

Dad was haemorrhaging from a hole in the wall of his oesophagus, a hole burned by decades of alcohol abuse. Pavla, married to a Greek doctor, phoned the ambulance and harangued them – two men more eager to spend their day off with their families – into driving an hour north to rescue the bleeding man. They thought it was a wild goose chase, she insisted they go anyway. She saved my dad's life. And then, in a less literal way, she saved mine.

As the ambulance took my dad to the hospital in Corfu town, my sister and I flew from Dublin to Heathrow, Heathrow to Athens, Athens to Corfu, cursing the winter flight schedule and, if I'm honest, cursing Dad for moving somewhere so inconvenient. 'Typical,' we muttered under our breath, keenly aware of the betrayal.

When we arrived at the hospital we were greeted with chaotic scenes – no information desk, patients smoking in the foyer, whole families camping in the common areas. After stalking several corridors, we finally found Dad, mercifully still alive. He was weak and slipping in and out of consciousness as we set up a vigil at his bedside.

It soon became apparent that we were alone. There were no doctors that we could find, and barely any nurses. What staff we saw were harried and couldn't speak English. One man visiting another patient leaned over to me and said in a thick accent, 'Without your family here, you die.' And faced with the haemorrhage and huge loss of blood, it seemed that Dad might die anyway, even if we were there.

We spent a lot of time in that hospital, waiting. Sitting on hard hospital chairs waiting for the doctor, waiting for the prognosis, waiting for the man with the clipboard, waiting for the nurse with the blood tests, waiting for the answers. Each appointment, each ritual, seemed to promise something – to bring us closer to the longed-for result, for somebody to say Dad would live. There were times I wanted to scream, and kick my heels, to demand that someone tell me the truth. But the truth is an impossible commodity in a hospital. And then there were times I thought, 'Just give me the bad news,' so great was my need for a definite answer.

But you can't spend your life just waiting. And that's when Pavla showed up. After we'd been observing our vigil a few days, Pavla came to the hospital, we shook hands and then hugged, her coat damp from the rain that seemed to fall constantly. In contrast, I felt paper dry. She translated for us with the nurse, who, after Pavla's cajoling words, was decidedly nicer to us all. Pavla roused Dad from his slumber, and even made him smile, relieving the tension for all of us with her simple normality.

And then she invited us for lunch. 'Oh no,' we said, 'we can't possibly leave him.' But she told us that leaving for a few hours would be good for us, we had to eat after all, and she reassured us that he would be there when we came back. Her certainty persuaded us.

We went to lunch in her apartment. It was warm and brightly lit. Her husband and children came and went. The food was good and filling. We tried to be less like strangers. To remember our manners. To remember how just to be.

After lunch we went back to the hospital, and I probably imagined it, but Dad seemed better. After being outside, the room seemed stale, so I opened a window and pressed my face to the fresh air. The next night we met Pavla for dinner. The night after that, others of Dad's friends invited us to their house for a meal. 'It's only an ordinary supper,' they said when we professed our gratitude. But it wasn't ordinary to us. It was life-saving.

Our first night in the hospital, a patient in the next room died. His relatives keened for him. I stood by the door of Dad's room, just listening, unable to move. It is hard to remember now the emotions that I felt at this realisation; it was as if, though my dad had not been the one to die, when I heard the screaming, I imagined myself to be the one yelling and crying at the injustice and the fear and the ineffable darkness of it all.

But now I look back, now that Dad is better, now that he hasn't had a drink in over five years, and I realise I have taken something else with me from that time, another kind of memory, another kind of emotion.

When Dad got sick, he called for help. That call was answered. And sometimes that's all you need. To know that you can call out, and someone who cares will answer.

Irish Water

Veronica Dyas

'If it's not one thing it's another,' she says, handing back the lottery ticket she's just checked and found wanting.

'Sure you'd never be finished,' the woman answers.

I'm standing slightly back and at an angle feeling impatient but smiling just in case anyone might think I'm being rude observing a conversation to which I'm not a part, I'm not party to it but I am standing here so it's only polite to smile.

'The party's over as the fella says,' an older man shouts over from the deli counter. The woman waves her lottery ticket in the air replying, 'I wasn't at that feckin' party.'

'None of us were,' says the woman behind the counter, 'how are the young people supposed to manage, no wonder they're leaving, sure they've nowhere to live.'

'Nowhere to live?' the older man answers moving nearer. 'Sure they won't even have water soon the way things are going.'

'Imagine, and we on an island, sure it never stops raining,' the woman answers.

'The sea, oh the sea is the gradh geal mo croide / Long may she stay between England and me / It's a sure guarantee that some hour we'll be free / Oh, thank God we're surrounded by water,' the man sings, paying for his corned beef and sauntering out the door.

I smile again, feeling awkward now standing waiting to buy my tobacco. I'm glad I don't smoke anymore. But it leaves ye with time on your hands that you didn't know you were wasting before. I wasn't prepared for that. It's not just what to do with the hands is the issue, it's where to be putting yourself generally, that full ninety-odd minutes spread out over the day that's no longer taken up with rolling tobacco and smoking it.

Out on the street it's bitter, it's a bitter cold day in winter, the kind of one that you'd go to the pictures to get in out of, if you could afford to. It's the kind of day that your granny used to make stew on, no point stewing on that now either I suppose.

We are gathering now, our little Liberties contingent, pooling up on the street outside the Little Flower Hall, trickling round onto Thomas Street then streaming down Oliver Bond Hill, where Robert Emmet's head rolled down after he was hung, drawn and quartered, they told us.

There's many's a thing they told us then that I think twice on now, I ponder, looking back up the hill at our little group, mulling on all the other little groups gathering across the country above the underground rivers constantly flowing beneath our feet.

We're gathering momentum coming down the hill and over the bridge southside to north like a waterfall cascading after the rushes and there they are, coming up from Heuston Station, up the quays. Up from Kerry, from Cork, Clare, Waterford, Donegal.

From all over the country they're coming, echoing what we're saying ourselves, only we're a bit quieter because we're too busy chatting away to each other.

It's friendly, buoyant even, with smiles and salutations and 'Ah jaysus I haven't seen you for ages, how are ye doin'?' kind of pockets of people arriving. Children in buggies and on backs and held close over hips and holding banners they made themselves at home with their parents.

'Great to see so many here isn't it?'

'Ah it's amazing altogether.'

We are gathering now, each subsidiary collecting itself into the whole.

Across the crowd I see a group of older men in overcoats with medals pinned on to them. I don't know them, but somehow I recognise their importance, their lined faces on tree-trunk torsos staring stoic, there's something solid about them, even against the

frailty of their age. A man in a wheelchair is pushed along with the crowd, a child on his lap holding a banner, two women and their dog walk nonchalantly but with purpose.

And then the calm comes. The turbulent bubbly beginning shifts into the maturity of the ancient flow of water along the Liffey.

One entity, we shift into step.

The slow but steady pace of a hundred thousand people walking their own lands.

Chanting and listening and walking and talking at the same time. 'I tell ye I've never seen anything like it, not since the hunger strikes.'

We move in simultaneous formation, in tandem with our differences, our politics might never be the same again, but today we'll stand together.

We. Us. Together.

We can see each other again now, we can see each other now, again.

We're still here, I think. We're still here.

The Sea, the Sea

John F. Deane

We would sit sometimes, late evenings, in the kitchen of the old house, Bunnacurry, Achill Island, listening to storms gathering off the Atlantic. Grannie would weep, because her son, a ship's engineer, would be out on the high seas; the winds howled in the chimney and filled the kitchen with sorry apprehension. But other times, on a warm summer day, we swam in the sheltered cove in Dooega where Grannie would lean her old back against a rock and allow the small waves to caress her feet. Mother held me carefully, her hands under my back, urging me to float, to trust the sea to bear me up and, when I overcame my fear of the waves and the jellyfish, I abandoned myself with delight to the experience. I came to respect and wonder at the vastness of the sea, and at the potency of the love that held me safe.

Father, too, urged us on to sea things: we fished alongside him, spinning from the rocks at the base of cliffs on Achill where we were sometimes in danger of being carried away by a freak, high-flying wave. The sea, the sea; I read in Isaiah these words: 'They lift up their voices, they sing for joy; they shout from the west over the majesty of the Lord. Therefore in the east give glory to the Lord; in the islands of the sea glorify the name of the Lord.' The sea, then, has ghosted my living, with its moods, its power, its sources of innocent pleasures.

Later on, when I saw my father stand by the ocean in his old age, aware of the diminishments the years can bring to the human frame, I sorrowed to see how he longed to, but could not, go in for a swim. I watched him as, slightly embarrassed, he took off shoes and socks,

rolled up his trousers to his knees, paddled his lily-white legs in the lesser waves of the great ocean. So much, then, of sea and sky and island, has left its caul in my flesh and soul that I come always to the shore to scavenge for some understanding. Around me, the black-backs watch, sharp-eyed and silent, shuffling on the stones or strand, like monks restless in choir.

In September 2015 I went with my wife Ursula to the island of Crete. The holiday crowds were already leaving and we found a sheltered bay and swam in the clear, warm waters of the Mediterranean. Crete, too, holds its memories of the sad histories of man's inhumanity to man. In the monastery at Arkadi, three monks remain, the rich catholicon holding relics of the priests' resistance to the Ottomans many years ago. In the dim church we knelt, praying for the new century unfolding in its outlandish ways, knowing at times how we are halt, how we butt against the limitations of our hopes. There was still an aftertaste of summer; the harbour was musical with the tinkling bells of yachts and the silver-trumpet sparkle of the sun.

In another Orthodox monastery, Preveli, hung between earth and heaven, among the scorched, bare-knuckle mountains of Crete, there are memorials to warrior monks who smuggled their allied soldiers down precipitous cliffs to the sea to escape the Nazi onslaught. Church militant. The monks still hold the fortress for their God, live in dusty black; like eagles they soar on the mountain flanks, the sea far below them, innocent in a heavenly blue.

One evening we sat on the terrace of a restaurant, watching out over the gentlest of seas, enjoying a warm Cretan red wine. Earlier that day, I had taken off my shoes and socks, rolled up my trousers and waded cautiously in the shallower water, embarrassed at the lily-white smoothness of my legs. We saw, on television, the body of a three-year-old boy, lying face down on a beach, lost at sea in his family's flight from the wars in Syria. Alan Kurdi, refugee, red T-shirt, short-sleeved; navy blue shorts, shoes navy blue. The Mediterranean appeared to have repented of its wildness and carried that small body on its back, gently, ashore; he lay, face down, on the wet shingles. How shall we forgive, how shall we be forgiven? The sea, the sea; it holds within itself so much of our human folly and misery. If we, unhurried, pause a while to listen, down by the shore, we may hear that child, and so many more, drawing in a long, slow sigh, then a quiet out-breathing, and a pause, before, once more, that long, slow sigh.

I Was Full of Wine
When the Call Came

John Kelly

I was full of wine when the call came.
Our kids and the neighbours' kids
were all dolled-up like zombies –
stitched-up corpses with white faces,
black eyeliner and fake blood.
On the floor, a red plastic basin
swayed like small, woozy sea –
bits of floating apple already turning brown,
dishcloths soaking up the spill.
No need to ruin it, I thought.
Tomorrow would be time enough.
I put a black tie in my pocket and I left.

Halloween. A night I used to love.
Sweaty false-faces from Wellworths,
Fanta, fruit and monkey nuts.
And though I couldn't name it then,
that thrilling rip in everything as spirits,
manes and shades walked abroad on our estates.
I wore a vampire's cloak my mother made
from the blackout curtain that saved Eden Street
from the Luftwaffe in 1941.
The undead cast no shadow, or so they said,

but mine was on the footpath, arms spread wide.
And I loved the flowing, phantom shape of me in flight.

So, as Halloween slipped into All-Saints,
and my mother slipped closer to her death,
I, not fit to drive, was on the last bus north,
forced by its own sobering schedule
onto old forgotten roads, turning hard
into bypassed places like Navan and Cavan and Kells.
That slow crow over Dalkey, I kept thinking,
and a week of not sleeping and bad dreams.
And all the time my mother, who never drank or smoked,
was hooked up on something (morphine?)
in the South West Acute. Adrenalin too, they told me later,
keeping her on earth until I got there.

The driver was a speed merchant.
Like a man who'd left the immersion on
he blarged on through the black beyond Belturbet
and up and over the vanished border.
I imagined a mountain pass in Transylvania
and him lashing at his horses in a thunderstorm,
our caleche hurtling to the land beyond the forest.
Or else a long-haul flight at night in heavy turbulence,
when you check the screen to see where you are,
and you're somewhere over Syria or Iraq
and up ahead, it's Mosul and Baghdad.
Nothing but mad drivers, she'd have said.

They say that hearing is the last to go,
so she'd have heard the slowing, vital beeps,
my questions and the nurses' sympathetic chat –
all that talk of screens and dropping numbers
as the body persevered.
A heart like a lion, the nurse behind me said,

but, in the end, my mother held my hands
as if to teach the toddler me to walk,
or perhaps to join her in a dance.
And in the middle of all the mystery
and the no-great-mystery of death,
I was still afraid she'd smell the Merlot on my breath.

Ophelia of Ballybough

Jessica Traynor

Motherhood leaves me like a wire stripped of its casing. In the low-slung sun of October I walk, newborn baby in sling, the sun glinting on the copper of my filament.

They're not unpleasant, these mid-autumn days of first maternity leave, adjusting to the movement of that solid weight from my womb to the sling on my front, the embrace of the sling's earthquake-proof straps. The baby struggles, then sleeps, as I walk a slow circuit. Clonliffe Road, Drumcondra Road, Richmond Road, Fairview Strand, Fairview Park. I feel a little ghostlike, like Ophelia in a spectacle in a Pre-Raphaelite painting. As I walk, new things reveal themselves. Wild things. Magpies. Treecreepers. Grey squirrels. A stalking heron. On the playing fields beside the Tolka, a flock of Canada geese.

I remember the documentary I'd watched about a man who had adopted and raised a flock of wild turkeys. As they imprinted on him and walked longer and longer through the wilderness, other animals stopped seeing the man as a threat. They stopped seeing him at all. New motherhood can feel like this. Like you've been kinked a little closer to the wild. Like the bones of your house might reject you as a sudden alien incumbent.

And like something feral, like a stripped wire, I'm all nerve. The world has stolen my skin and suddenly everything can get in.

Through all this, the baby is content, well fed, learning the corners of her body by slow, torturous increments. I hold her like some marvellous fish I've poached from a river; terrified she might slip from my grasp, terrified that she won't be able to survive this strange new element.

In the midst of all these terrors, I fashion small moments of love. On a golden day in October as she sleeps against my chest, I sing 'Lavender's Blue' standing on the empty football pitch on Richmond Road. I cross the Luke Kelly bridge and describe to her the snowy egrets picking their way through the tidal mud. In a moment so surreal I doubt its reality, two kingfishers burst from beneath the bridge, livid jewels cast against the river's flow, past flashing sludge-encrusted tyres to the far willow trees. The baby sleeps through it all, but I see it for her, record these symbols, this slight slippage in the order of things that allows me such special vision. I think of Ophelia in her madness, seeing the darkness of the world with such clarity, but only able to communicate through the symbolism of flowers: fennel, columbine, pansy, rue.

The weather turns. The public-health nurse calls to ask how I am doing. I have been placed on a high-risk list for postnatal depression, because beside a statement on a questionnaire asking *Have you felt overwhelmed since the birth?* I ticked *Yes*. This is a source of some personal embarrassment, and I find myself reassuring the nurse each time she comes. But still, although I am doing well, there is a niggling sense of something dangerous in this skinless, feral, interior life. The public-health nurse reminds me Storm Ophelia is on her way. How apt.

My partner comes home and we camp in our kitchen with pots of coffee. The baby snoozes in her bouncy chair, still adjusting to her new element. We expect flying wheelie bins, the train from the railway line above our house to come careening off its track, bicycles and cars to soar past us like a scene from *The Wizard of Oz*. But though the breeze is high, the silence of our high-walled back yard is oppressive. At one point I almost consider taking the baby on her daily walk, before news of fatalities comes through on the radio. I sit down again, pour another coffee. We weather the day without damage.

The next day, I wheel the pram through Fairview Park, skirting the limbs of fallen trees. A beech tree blocks my path and I stop to look at it, intrigued by the strange privilege of this view – the private mysteries of its root-ball coughed up. Its prone shape makes me think again of Ophelia toppled, carried away by water beneath over-hanging willows. For some, I think, the very worst thing has happened. For some, but not, today, for me. I wheel the baby home. The days may have darkened into winter since then, may have lost their strange electric gleam. But I'm no longer feral, no longer Ophelia's ghost cursed to haunt my town speaking in symbols. Those filaments that split after my daughter's birth have begun to form into a new identity. I am, among other things, a mother.

NOTES ON CONTRIBUTORS

Kevin Barry is author of the novels *Night Boat to Tangier, Beatlebone* and *City of Bohane* and the story collections *Dark Lies the Island* and *There Are Little Kingdoms*.

Denise Blake's third collection of poetry, *Invocation* was published by Revival Press. She facilitates creative writing workshops in schools through Poetry Ireland Writers in Schools, CAP Poetry in Motion and she also works with adult groups. www.deniseblake.com

John Boland is a poet and critic. He has written for the *Irish Press* and *The Irish Times* and is currently television critic and book reviewer with the *Irish Independent*.

Dermot Bolger is a poet, novelist and playwright. His latest novel, *An Ark of Light*, was published in 2018. His new play, *Last Orders at the Dockside*, will be premiered by the Abbey Theatre in 2019. In 1988 he was editor of Raven Arts Press, which he ran between 1979 and 1992.

Pat Boran was born in Portlaoise and lives in Dublin where he works in literary publishing. He has published a dozen books of poetry and prose, most recently the poetry collection *Then Again*. He is a member of Aosdána.

John Bowman is a broadcaster and historian. He has been engaged in current affairs and historical broadcasting on RTÉ Radio and television since the 1960s. His books include *De Valera and the Ulster Question, 1917–1973, Window and Mirror: RTÉ Television 1961–2011* and *Ireland: The Autobiography*.

Bernadett Buda is Hungarian, living in Ireland. She is fascinated by languages and writing, studied English at master's level and is a qualified language teacher. She has devoted more time to writing thanks to the inspirational pieces she heard on *Sunday Miscellany*.

Honor Clynes is a Dubliner, a decade older than *Sunday Miscellany* and a lifelong fan of the programme. She is married to Martin, with four children, Aedín, Peter, Isolde and Róisín and a retriever, Vega. She is a language enthusiast *agus múinteoir Gaeilge do dhaoine fásta* on a 'leisure and pleasure' basis.

Evelyn Conlon is the author of four novels and three collections of short stories and has edited four anthologies. Her work has been widely anthologised and translated. Books Upstairs have re-published *A Glassful of Letters and Telling*, which was translated into Chinese in 2019.

John Connell is an award-winning author, film-maker, journalist and farmer. He is the author of the number-one bestseller *The Cow Book*. He lives and farms in County Longford.

Leo Cullen's books includes the short story collection *Let's Twist Again* and the novel *Clocking Ninety on the Road to Cloughjordan*. He has published in journals, newspapers, and magazines and broadcast on RTÉ Radio and BBC Radio 4.

Gerald Dawe is a Belfast-born poet who has published over twenty volumes of poetry and literary criticism including *Mickey Finn's Air* and *The Last Peacock*. He was professor of English and Fellow of Trinity College Dublin until his retirement in 2017. *The Wrong Country: Essays on Modern Irish Writing* was published in 2018. He lives in Dún Laoghaire.

John F. Deane was born on Achill Island, Co. Mayo. He is founder of Poetry Ireland and the *Poetry Ireland Review*. In 2018 he published *Dear Pilgrims* and *Achill: The Island*, a book of poems illustrated by John Behan RHA. He has been poet in residence at Boston College and at Loyola University, Chicago.

Louis de Paor has been involved with the renaissance of contemporary poetry in Irish since 1980 when he was first published in the poetry journal *Innti*, which he subsequently edited. A four-times winner of the Oireachtas prize for the best collection of poems in Irish, he lived in Australia from 1987 to 1996. His most recent collections are *The Brindled Cat and the Nightingale's Tongue* and *Grá Fiar*.

Martina Devlin is an author and journalist. Her latest book is *Truth & Dare*, a short-story collection, while her novels include *About Sisterland* and *The House Where It Happened*. She writes a weekly current affairs column for the *Irish Independent* and is a PhD candidate at Trinity College Dublin.

Veronica Dyas is an artist working primarily through theatre, new text and installation. Her theatre work includes *HERE AND NOW (I live here now)*, *In My Bed, My Son, My Son* and *N.E.S. in a Noose*.

Mia Gallagher is an award-winning novelist and short-story writer. Her books include the novels *HellFire* (2006), *Beautiful Pictures of the Lost Homeland* (2016) and her debut story collection, *Shift*. She is a member of Aosdána.

Sinéad Gleeson is a writer and the editor of three short-story anthologies, including *The Long Gaze Back*. Her debut book of essays is *Constellations* (2019). She is the 2019 Writer-in-Residence at UCD.

Conall Hamill was born in Dublin and grew up in Clontarf. He was educated at St Joseph's CBS and Trinity College Dublin. A teacher of English and French, he co-founded the St Andrew's College One-Act Theatre Festival and has acted with Co-Motion Theatre.

Donal Hayes is a writer and radio documentary-maker living in Kinsale. He has broadcast on RTÉ, CBC and C103 and been published in the *Irish Examiner, The Irish Times, Literary Orphans, Newer York* and online. He is happiest with a biro in hand, staring out the window.

Robert Higgins is an award-winning writer from Longford represented by the Marianne Gunn O'Connor Agency. He was nominated for the Hennessy Award in 2014. He recently wrote and directed his first short film, which is currently touring film festivals. His debut play *The Streets Are Ours* recently completed a national tour.

Alannah Hopkin is a novelist, travel writer and critic. Her story collection *The Dogs of Inishere* was published in 2017. She reviews regularly for the *Irish Examiner* and contributes to the Irishwoman's Diary in *The Irish Times*.

Cyril Kelly was born in Listowel in 1945. He taught in Arklow for a year and then in Coolock, Dublin, until his early retirement in 2001. He is married, with three adult daughters and, as of now, 5.5 grandsons.

John Kelly's poetry has appeared in numerous journals and anthologies. A debut collection, *Notions,* was published by Dedalus Press in 2018.

Anne Marie Kennedy is an award-winning writer, performance poet, creative-writing tutor and freelance journalist. She lives in south Galway with her husband and a menagerie of four-legged people.

Claire Kilroy is the author of the novels novels *The Devil I Know, All Names Have Been Changed, All Summer* and *Tenderwire* and the recipient of the 2004 Rooney Prize for Irish Literature. She lives in Dublin.

Caitriona Lally received the 2018 Rooney Prize for Irish Literature. Her debut novel, *Eggshells,* was shortlisted for the Newcomer Award at the 2015 Bórd Gais Irish Book Awards and the Kate O'Brien Debut Novel Award the following year. She was the featured writer at *Starboard Home*, a celebration of Dublin Port in the National Concert Hall in 2016.

Mae Leonard is from Limerick and now resides in Co. Kildare. She is a long-time contributor to *Sunday Miscellany* and her stories have been broadcast and widely. A retired swimming teacher, she also enjoys being a writer in schools.

Brian Leyden was born in Arigna in Co. Roscommon and has written extensively about his home area for *Sunday Miscellany*. His current publications are *Sweet Old World: New & Selected Stories,* his memoir *The Home Place,* and the novel *Summer of '63.*

John MacKenna is the author of nineteen books and a dozen stage plays. He teaches creative writing at NUIM and lives in Co. Carlow. He has been a regular contributor to *Sunday Miscellany* for a decade.

Siobhán Mannion has won awards for short fiction and radio drama. Her writing has appeared in *Granta, Winter Papers, Stand, Banshee* and *The Long Gaze Back* and elsewhere. She is currently completing a first collection of stories.

Rosaleen McDonagh is a playwright from the Travelling community.

Lisa McInerney's work has featured in *Winter Papers, The Stinging Fly, Granta, The Guardian,* on BBC Radio 4 and in many anthologies. Her story 'Navigation' was longlisted for the 2017 *Sunday Times* EFG Short Story Award. Her debut novel, *The Glorious Heresies,* won the 2016 Baileys Women's Prize for Fiction and the 2016 Desmond Elliott Prize. Her second novel, *The Blood Miracles,* won the 2018 RSL Encore Award.

Danielle McLaughlin's stories have been broadcast on RTÉ Radio 1 and BBC Radio 4 and published in *The Stinging Fly, The Irish Times, Southword* and *The New Yorker.* She edited *Counterparts,* an anthology of work by writers with legal back-grounds published in aid of Peter McVerry Trust. She won the Windham-Campbell Prize in 2019.

Janet Moran is an actor and writer living in Dublin. She co-wrote the play *Swing* and more recently wrote *A Holy Show,* which premiered at the Peacock Theatre as part of Dublin Fringe and toured both nationally and internationally in 2019.

Mary Morrissy is the author of three novels, *Mother of Pearl, The Pretender* and *The Rising of Bella Casey* and two collections of stories, *A Lazy Eye* and *Prosperity Drive.* She is Associate Director of Creative Writing at University College Cork and a member of Aosdána.

Colin Murphy is a playwright and journalist. His play *Haughey/Gregory* is published by Methuen Drama and is one of a series of plays he has written on Irish political history that have been produced by Fishamble: The New Play Company. He has also written essays for *The Dublin Review.*

Éilís Ní Dhuibhne was born in Dublin. She is a novelist, short-story writer, playwright and literary critic and writes in both Irish and English. Her latest books are *Selected Stories* and a memoir, *Twelve Thousand Days.* Awards include a shortlisting for the Orange Prize for Fiction, the Irish Pen Award for an Outstanding Contribution to Irish Literature in 2015 and a Hennessy Hall of Fame Award for Lifetime Achievement in 2016. She has been Writer Fellow in UCD and Trinity College and is a member of Aosdána.

Doireann Ní Ghríofa is a bilingual writer whose books explore birth, death, desire, and domesticity. Her awards include a Lannan Fellowship and the Ostana Prize. She is a member of Aosdána.

Joseph O'Connor was born in Dublin. He is the author of nine novels including *Star of the Sea*, *Ghost Light*, *Shadowplay*, and a number of stage plays and non-fiction books. Among his awards are the Prix Zepter for European Novel of the Year. His work has been translated into forty languages. He is McCourt Professor of Creative Writing at the University of Limerick.

Nuala O'Connor's books include the novel *Becoming Belle* (2018) and the short-story collection *Joyride to Jupiter* (2017). 'Gooseen', which won the UK's 2018 Short Fiction Prize, was published in *Granta* and shortlisted for Story of the Year at the Irish Book Awards 2019. www.nualaoconnor.com

Simon Ó Faoláin has published three poetry collections. His awards include Duais Glen Dimplex, Duais Strong, Duais Bhaitéar Uí Mhaicín, Duais Cholm Cille and Duais Foras na Gaeilge. His latest book is *An Corrmhíol*, an Irish-language translation of the Scots-Gaelic long poem *A' Mheanbhchuileag* by Fearghas MacFionnlaigh.

Melatu Uche Okorie is from Nigeria and has been living in Ireland for over twelve years. Her short-story collection, *This Hostel Life*, was published by Skein Press in 2018 and her stories have appeared in numerous anthologies. She has an MPhil in creative writing from Trinity College Dublin.

Michael O'Loughlin was born in Dublin in 1958. Having living abroad for many years he returned to Dublin in 2002. He has published six collections of poetry as well as criticism, translations and essays, and has written screenplays for feature films. He is a regular contributor to *The Irish Times* and *Sunday Miscellany*. He is a member of Aosdána.

Mary O'Malley is from Co. Galway. She has published seven poetry collections as well as books of criticism, translations, essays and screenplays. Her poems have been widely translated. She is a member of Aosdána.

Karl O'Neill was born in Armagh and is now based in Dublin. He is a professional actor and writer, author of a children's book, stage plays and several radio plays for RTÉ. A frequent contributor to *Sunday Miscellany*, his work has appeared in *Grist, Krino, The Irish Times* and *The Irish Catullus*. He is currently working on a book of his children's stories.

Emilie Pine is Associate Professor of Modern Drama at the School of English, Drama and Film, University College Dublin. Emilie has published widely as an academic and critic. Her first collection of personal essays, *Notes to Self*, was the recipient of the 2018 Butler Literary Award.

Liam Power is a Kilkenny man, living in Kill, Co. Kildare. A member of Scribblers Writers' Group, he has recently self-published *Liam's Tales and Trails* and his writing has appeared in *Ireland's Own*. He enjoys travel, social dancing and reading. He has volunteered for the Senior Help Line and as an Adult Literacy Tutor. He is a member of Lucan Toastmasters.

Paul Rouse is a professor of history at University College Dublin. He has written extensively about the history of sport and about Irish history. His latest book, *The Hurlers*, was published by Penguin in 2018.

Barbara Scully is a writer and broadcaster from Cabinteely, and is regularly published in newspapers and magazines. She contributes to a variety of programmes on Newstalk Radio and Virgin Media TV. She has three adult daughters and a granddaughter and describes herself as 'a slave to four cats and owner of an elderly deaf dog'. She has one husband and cares for a family of urban foxes in her garden.

Denis Sexton was born in Dublin but has mostly lived elsewhere. He is a winner of RTÉ's P.J. O'Connor Award for Radio Drama. RTÉ has also broadcast his radio plays, comedy scripts and *Sunday Miscellany* essays. He played the part of Fergus Dalton in *Fair City* and also practises as a graphologist.

Stephen James Smith is a Dublin poet and playwright, immersed in Dublin's spoken-word scene. His poetry videos have attracted millions of views. In 2017 he was commissioned by the St Patrick's Festival to write a new poem as a 'celebratory narrative' of Ireland: the result was 'My Ireland'. An accompanying short film was screened at the London Film Festival.

Gemma Tipton is a writer on arts and culture with *The Irish Times* and other publications including *Artforum*, *Frieze*, *Image* and *Cara*. Dividing her time between Dublin and Kinsale, she loves art, horses and music, and most recently was director of the Blackwater Valley Opera Festival.

Jessica Traynor's latest collection of poetry is *The Quick* (2018). Her debut collection, *Liffey Swim* (2014), was shortlisted for the Strong/Shine Award. She won the 2011 Listowel Poetry Prize, was named Hennessy New Irish Writer of the Year in 2013 and received the 2014 Ireland Chair of Poetry bursary. She is under commission by Galway 2020 to write a libretto.

Enda Wyley has published five collections of poetry, most recently *Borrowed Space, New and Selected Poems*, published by Dedalus Press. She was the inaugural winner of the Vincent Buckley Poetry Prize and the recipient of a Patrick and Katherine Kavanagh Fellowship. She is a member of Aosdána.

ACKNOWLEDGEMENTS

All projects require the imagination, support and cooperation of many to find shape and be brought to fruition.

First and foremost an enormous thanks is due to each of the artists – the writers, composers and performers who accepted our invitation to contribute to the *Miscellany50* concert.

The support of Tom McGuire, Head of RTÉ Radio 1 and Ann-Marie Power, Head of Arts and Culture, RTÉ, made all the difference to its realisation. The support of the Broadcasting Authority of Ireland has been integral to ensuring that the idea behind this project happened.

New Island has published the majority of the *Sunday Miscellany* anthologies. It has been my pleasure on this project to work with the team there, particularly with Aoife K. Walsh, the publisher's commissioning editor. Her attention to detail has been invaluable and she has made key suggestions along the way as well as introducing me to editor Djinn von Noorden and designer Catherine Gaffney whose work on the book has been integral to its delivery. Thanks also to Marcus Mac Conghail who proofread the pieces in the Irish language. New Island General Manager Mariel Deegan ensured everything was in order at every stage of progressing the book's publication.

I am most grateful to my RTÉ colleagues: my co-producers of *Miscellany50*, Aoife Nic Chormaic and Sarah Binchy; broadcasting coordinator and administrator Carolyn Dempsey; administrative support, Suzanne Young and Caroline Flanagan; sound engineer Ciarán Cullen and his assistant Damien Galligan; Editor of RTÉ Culture, Derek O'Connor, video and web production, John Bates; legal advice, Deirdre Ann Kelly. RTÉ's Communications, Marketing and Press people including Joseph Hoban, Neil O'Gorman, Laura Beatty, Amy O'Driscoll, Maureen Catterson, Jilly McDonagh and Ellen Leonard were invaluable; as well as RTÉ Archives staff, Bríd Dooley, Tina Byrne, Michael Talty, Pearl Quinn, Robert Canning, Jack Smith and Brian Rice, and photographer John Cooney. Thanks also to Bridget Bhreathnach, John Donohue, Miriam McGowan and Eugene Roche.

Enormous gratitude to the *Miscellany50* festival production manager Lucy Ryan; screen and lighting designer Eoin Kilkenny and administrative assistant Ciara Coyne. A particular thanks to photographer Paul McCarthy, who documented *Miscellany50*, the festival, and whose photographs feature here. Cillian Hayes was simply invaluable in ensuring the installation of the *Miscellany50* exhibition was possible. Cian O'Brien and the staff of the Project Arts Centre, where the *Miscellany50* radio festival weekend took place and was recorded for broadcast, were also central to its success. Thanks as always to Brian Fay and our fabulous pair Nóra and Eoghan for their inestimable support.

Finally, the esteemed presence of An tUachtarán Michael D. Higgins and Sabina Higgins, who attended the Sunday afternoon *Miscellany50* concert, added a particularly special sparkle through their presence for its contributors and audience alike. Thanks for this addition to the celebration to Conor Ó Rathallaigh and Thérèse O'Connor in the Office of the President.

IMAGE CREDITS